Latin America
in the Nineteenth Century

A Selected Bibliography of Books
of Travel and Description
Published in English

by

A. CURTIS WILGUS

The Scarecrow Press, Inc.
Metuchen, N.J.   1973

Library of Congress Cataloging in Publication Data

Wilgus, Alva Curtis, 1897–
    Latin America in the nineteenth century.

    1. Latin America—Description and travel—
Bibliography. I. Title.
Z1601.W686   016.918'04'3   73–6891
ISBN 0–8108–0634–7

For

Karna

mi esposa

mi amiga

mi colaborador

TABLE OF CONTENTS

v

FOREWORD

Obadiah Rich has written: "Every author of a special bibliography must necessarily be much indebted to all those who have gone over the same ground before him, and his qualifications must be poor indeed if he does not improve upon the work of his predecessor."

No bibliography is ever complete or definitive. One remembers the bibliographer who listed all the books on a certain subject except the one he sat on everyday. Compiling bibliographies can be fun as well as work. It is a game of hide and seek, with some discovered facts of a "believe it or not" nature. It can be challenging and certainly rewarding. It can be frustrating and very time consuming. A reviewer can safely criticize a bibliography on the grounds of its being incomplete, or too selective, or unimportant, or uncritical, or unannotated, or inaccurate, or hastely compiled, or a waste of time of both the compiler and the reader. But these tools have long been prepared and will continue to be--until a computer takes over the task--for a bibliography is the beginning of wisdom on any subject and it opens doors into many areas. However, in using a bibliography, let the reader beware, for who knows what good--or evil--may lurk in such a guide?

My interest in books of travel and description relating to the Americas began as a graduate student, first at Madison and then at Berkeley. But this was only a half-hearted and indifferent interest for many years, during which time I purchased an increasing number of such accounts. Finally, after giving up numerous university responsibilities, I was able to devote serious effort to the search for items in dealers' catalogs, publishers' lists, second-hand book stores, and private and public libraries here and abroad. To begin with, I naively thought that I might find three or four hundred such books published originally in English or in English translation. But I found nearly that many "pamphlets," which I here define as less than 100 pages. As I continued my search, my surprise

and pleasure increased. With critical judgments, elimina-
tions and refinements, I have here listed, without repetition
or cross-references, 1182 titles. This number includes
anonymous books grouped together at the end of the main
listing.

The expression "Latin America" here includes all
areas south of the United States as well as Bermuda and
the Bahamas to the east. I have construed "travel and
description" broadly, but on a selective basis which I believe I can justify, to include guide books, geographies,
some histories, diaries, letters, memoirs and reminiscences,
autobiographies, pertinent collections of private and public
documents and papers, and some relevant fiction. My cri-
teria for selection may be considered too broad, but I have
kept in mind the type of contemporary account which will
help the reader to understand the peoples and areas with
which the book deals.

Many nineteenth century books have long titles--some
with 25 or more words. Generally, I have given short
titles, when acceptable, and I have placed in brackets further
pertinent information needed to describe the book's contents.
Some books were published much later than the dated subject
matter, and a few appeared for the first time in the present
century. The place of publication of each book is given
when known, but sometimes this information is lacking. A
number of the books were published simultaneously in different places. Some editions were very small and the books
today are almost unknown and are excessively rare. Names
of publishers are often impossible to find, and they frequently
change from book to book, or from year to year, or from
edition to edition. Titles, too, many change with the editions, and in some cases the same book may appear in the
same year, or in a later year, with a different title. I
have attempted to give the date of first publication, and the
date of the most recent reprint when known. But here again
is a difficulty: some books are published without dates,
copyright and publication dates may differ, and while the
date of a later edition can be found, the date of the first is
not available. Pagination is often treated lightly by printers:
some use Roman and Arabic numerals, some use one or the
other, some numbering overlaps, and occasionally page numbers are omitted altogether, which necessitates actual page
counting. Authors' birth and death dates are very elusive.
Many dates are conflicting, but many more are impossible
to find. Undoubtedly the most frustrating fact with regard

to authors and editors concerns their names. Variation in spelling is common, initials rather than given names are used, pseudonyms are all too frequent, and the anonymous author is generally completely elusive. Where "facts" of any type are in doubt, I have used question marks.

I have, of course, been unable to examine all books listed, although many have passed through my hands, and I have at one time or another owned several hundred. No book has been omitted because it is inaccurate, or unscientific, or exaggerated, or semi-fiction, or even poetry--if the contemporary descriptions are in keeping with the facts and thus constitute original sources. Books about the Mexican War and the Spanish American War are chosen if they record experiences and observations regarding the local scene, especially places, peoples and customs. Many books show the authors' prejudices, whether political, religious, social, racial, cultural or national. Some authors did their "homework" before traveling abroad, and they described what they saw, or thought they saw, with candor and a fair degree of accuracy. Some writers wrote to inflate their egos, or to impress the folks back home, or to try to achieve a reputation. Most of the books were written for adults, but a few children's books are pertinent. Unfortunately, some are dull, but then, so were some of the authors. Even a bibliography can be dull, as some may consider this one.

All items are numbered consecutively and are listed alphabetically by the generally accepted spelling of the family name, or by the designated pseudonym. For a few items I have been unable to find complete data. Perhaps this information can be supplied by the reader who may have more information than I have. I am not too disappointed that I cannot find all of the bibliographical facts to make this work more complete, for I long ago learned that important omissions exist in the catalogs of the Library of Congress (and its Union Catalog), of the New York Public Library, of the Explorers Club Library of New York City, of the British Museum, and of many other public and private libraries which I have been allowed to use. Moreover, many bibliographical guides which I have examined have been disappointing. A number of these aids may be found at the end of this volume in the "Selected List of References Containing Information about Nineteenth Century Books and Authors." Perhaps I exaggerate, although I hope not, when I say that I believe I have cited about 90% of the books (of 100 pages or more) which are relevant to this bibliography.

ix

A few final words are in order. I am especially grate-
ful to the Tinker Foundation of New York City for providing a
grant to the Inter-American Bibliographical and Library Association (transmitted through the Seminar on the Acquisition of
Latin American Library Materials) for the purpose of com-
pleting this work. Full recognition, certainly, must be
given to the well known patience of many librarians, even if
they must here remain anonymous. I have been fortunate
in having the cooperation of Gilberto V. Fort of Miami Dade
Junior College Instructional Resources, who prepared the
Geographical Index. The chart showing the number of books
about Latin America published in the United States was prepared in my seminar at the George Washington University in
1945. The escape clause for all of these friends is: no
person or organization can be held responsible for any
errors, because they are my own.

A. Curtis Wilgus
Director Emeritus
School of Inter-American Studies
University of Florida

September 27, 1972

BIBLIOGRAPHY

A

1. ABBOT, Rev. Abiel (1770-1828)
   Letters Written in the Interior of Cuba... [Feb.
   May, 1828]. Boston: Bowles and Dearborn, 1829.
   256, 15p. (Reprinted: New York, Books for
   Libraries, 1971.)

2. ABBOT, John Stevens Cabot (1805-77)
   South and North: Impressions Received During a
   Trip to Cuba and the South [of U.S.]. New York:
   Abbey and Abbot, 1860. 352p. (Reprinted: New
   York, Negro Universities Press, 1969.)

3. ADALBERT, Prince (of Prussia) Heinrich Wilhelm
   (1811-73)
   Travels of His Royal Highness Prince Adalbert of
   Prussia [Brazil, 1842-43; Europe]. London: D.
   Bogue, 1849, 2 vols. (Tr. from German.)

4. ADAM, William Jackson
   Journal of Voyages to Marguaritta, Trinidad, and
   Maturin... [Venezuela, Bolivar, etc; 1819-20].
   Dublin: R.M. Tims, 1824. 160p.

5. ADAMS, C. B.
   Catalogue of Shells Collected at Panama, with
   Notes on their Synonymy, Station, and Geographical
   Distribution. New York: Privately Printed, 1852.
   342p.

6. ADAMS, James M.
   Pioneering in Cuba, A Narrative of the Settlement
   of La Gloria, the First American Colony in Cuba,
   and the Early Experiences of the Pioneers [late
   19th century]. Concord, N.H.: Rumford Press,
   1901. 220p.

1

7. AGASSIZ, Louis (1807-1873) and Elizabeth Cabot Cary
   Agassiz (1822-1907)
   A Journey in Brazil. Boston: Ticknor and Fields,
   1868. xx, 540p. (Reprinted: New York, Praeger,
   1969.)

8. AKERS, Charles Edmond (1861-1915)
   Argentine, Patagonian and Chilean Sketches with a
   few Notes on Uruguay. London: Harrison and
   Sons, 1893. 190p.

9. ALCARAZ, Ramón (editor and translator)
   The Other Side: or, Notes for the History of the
   War between the United States and Mexico. New
   York and London: J. Wiley, 1850. xvi, 458p.
   (Tr. from Spanish.)

10. ALCEDO, Capt. Antonio de
    Alcedo's Geographical and Historical Dictionary of
    America and the West Indies. London: James
    Carpinter, 1812-15. 5 volumes. xx, 574, 597,
    512, 636, xvi, 642p.

11. ALEXANDER, Sir James Edward (1803-85)
    Transatlantic Sketches [N. and S. America and
    West Indies]. London: R. Bentley, 1833. 2 vols.
    Philadelphia: Key and Biddle, 1833. 1 vol.
    378p; London, 1833, 2 volumes.

12. ANDERSON, Alexander Dwight
    Mexico from the Material Standpoint... [resources,
    etc.]. Washington and New York: A. Brentano,
    1884. 156p.

13. ANDERSON, Alexander Dwight
    The Silver Country; or, the Great Southwest [and
    Mexico]. New York: G. P. Putnam's Sons, 1877.
    221p.

14. ANDERSON, Richard Clough Jr.
    The Diary and Journal of...1814-1826 [Colombia].
    Durham: Duke University Press, 1964. xxx, 342p.
    (first edition, edited by Alfred Tischendorf and E.
    Taylor Parks.)

15. ANDERSON, Robert (1805-71)
    An Artillery Officer in the Mexican War. Letters

of... [1846-7]. New York: G. P. Putnam's Sons,
1911. xvi, 339p. (first edition, edited by daughter
Eva Anderson Lawton.)

16. ANDERSON, William Marshall (1807-81)
An American in Maximilian's Mexico, 1865-6.
San Marino: The Huntington Library, 1959.
xxxii, 132p. (first edition, edited by Ramón
Eduardo Ruiz.)

17. ANDREWS, Christopher Columbus (1829-1922)
Brazil. Its Condition and Prospects [1882-5].
New York: D. Appleton and Co., 1887. 352p.

18. ANDREWS, Capt. Joseph
Journey from Buenos Aires through the Provinces
of Córdova, Tucumán, and Salta to Potosí... [1825-
6]. London: John Murray, 1827. 2 vols. xxxii,
312, viii, 321p. (Reprinted: New York, A. M. S.
Press, 1971.)

19. ANDREWS, W. S.
Illustrations of the West Indies; Sailing Directions
for the Caribbean Sea, Gulf of Mexico and Florida
and Descriptions of Views [Mexico, Panama,
Colombia, Venezuela]. London: Day and Son,
1860. 2 vols. in 1.

20. APPLETON, Elizabeth Haven (1815-90)
Narrative of the Imprisonment and Escape of Capt.
Charles H. Brown from the Chilean Convicts
[1851]. Boston: George C. Rand, 1884. 228p.

21. ARAGO, Jacques (1790-1855)
Narrative of a Voyage Around the World, 1817-20
[Argentina, Brazil, Uruguay, etc.]. London:
Treuttell, 1823. vi, 410p.

22. ARGYLL, (Ninth) Duke of (1845-1914)
A Trip to the Tropics and Home through America
... [West Indies and Southern United States].
London: Hurst and Blackett, 1867. 2nd edition.
xii, 355p.

23. ARMITAGE, John (1807-56)
History of Brazil [1808-31; with personal observa-
tions]. London: Smith, Elder and Co., 1836.

2 vols. 386, 306p. (continuation of Southey.)
(Reprinted: New York, A.M.S. Press, 1971.)

24. ARTHUR, Col. George
The Defense of the Settlers of Honduras... [his
correspondence, 1820-3]. Jamaica: A. Aikman,
1824. 101p. (Reprinted: Westport, Negro Universities Press, 1971.)

25. ASHE, Thomas (1770-1835)
A Commercial View and Geographical Sketch of
the Brazils in South America. London: Allen
and Co., 1812. 160p.

26. (ASSU), Jacaré
Brazilian Colonization from an European Point of
View. London: Edward Stanford, 1873. 132p.

27. ATCHISON, Charles C.
A Winter Cruise in Summer Seas. Diary of a
Two Month's Voyage in the R.M.S.P. Company's
S.S. Clyde through the Brazils to Buenos Aires
and Back for 100 pounds. London: Sampson Low,
Marston and Co., 1891. xxx, 399p.

28. ATKINS, John Black
The War in Cuba [an Englishman's experiences
with the U.S. Army]. London: Smith, Elder and
Co., 1899. x, 291p.

29. AUBERTIN, John James (1818-1900)
A Fight with Distance [Cuba, Bahamas, Canada,
etc.]. London: K. Paul, Trench and Co., 1888.
352p.

30. AUBERTIN, John James
A Flight to Mexico. London: K. Paul, Trench
and Co., 1882. 325p.

31. AUBERTIN, John James
By Order of the Sun. To Chile to see the Total
Eclipse April 16, 1893 [and Peru, Bolivia].
London: Kegan Paul, Trench and Trübner, 1894.
152p.

32. AUDUBON, John James (1785-1851)
Audubon's Western Journal, 1849-50 [including

Mexican territory]. Cleveland: Clark, 1906.
249p.

B

33. (BACHE, Richard) (1794-1836)
    Notes on Colombia Taken in the Years 1822-23...
    [by U. S. Army soldier]. Philadelphia: H. C.
    Carey and I. Lea, 1827. 303p.

34. BACON, Edgar Mayhew (1855-1935) and Eugene Mur-
    ray Aaron
    The New Jamaica.... New York: Walbridge and
    Co., 1890. xii, 243p.

35. BAEDEKER, Earl (editor)
    The United States with an Excursion into Mexico.
    Handbook for Travelers. New York: Scribner's,
    1893. 516p. (Revised edition, 1899, 579p.)
    (Reprinted: New York: Da Capo, 1971; 1893
    edition.)

36. BAILY, John (fl. 1811-50)
    Central America, Describing each of the States
    of Guatemala, Honduras, Salvador, Nicaragua and
    Costa Rica. London: Trelawney Saunders, 1850.
    xii, 164p.

37. BAIRD, Robert (1798-1863)
    Impressions and Experiences in the West Indies
    and North America in 1849. Edinburgh: W.
    Blackwood and Sons, 1850, 2 volumes; Philadel-
    phia: Lea and Blanchard, 1850. 354p.

38. BAKER, Frank Collins (b. 1867)
    A Naturalist in Mexico [and Cuba]. Chicago:
    D. Oliphant, 1895. 145p.

39. BAKER, John Martin
    A View of the Commerce between the United
    States and Rio de Janeiro. Washington: Demo-
    cratic Review, 1838. 118p.

40. BALDWIN, John Denison (1809-83)
    Ancient America [history and description]. New
    York: Harper and Brothers, 1872. 299p.

41. BALL, John (1818-89)
     Notes of a Naturalist in South America [Peru,
     Chile, Argentina, Uruguay, Brazil]. London:
     Kegan Paul, Trench, 1887. xiii, 416p.

42. BALLENTINE, George (b. 1812)
     The Mexican War, by an English Soldier [auto-
     biography and adventures with the United States
     Army]. New York: W. A. Townsend and Co.,
     1860. xii, 288p. (first published in U. S. Army
     Magazine.)

43. BALLOU, Maturin Murray (1820-95)
     Aztec Land [Mexico, description]. Boston:
     Houghton, Mifflin Co., 1890. x, 355p.

44. BALLOU, Maturin Murray
     Due South, or Cuba Past and Present. Boston:
     Houghton, Mifflin Co., 1885. x, 316p. (Reprinted:
     Westport, Negro Universities Press, 1971.)

45. BALLOU, Maturin Murray
     Equatorial America... [West Indies and South
     America]. Boston: Houghton, Mifflin and Co.,
     1892. x, 371p.

46. BALLOU, Maturin Murray
     History of Cuba, or Notes of a Traveler in the
     Tropics. Boston: Phillips, Sampson and Co.,
     1854. viii, 230p. (also New York, 1854.) (Re-
     printed: New York, A. M. S. Press, 1972.)

47. BANCROFT, Dr. Edward Nathaniel (1772-1842)
     A Letter to the Commissioners of Military Inquiry
     [British Caribbean, 1811-42]. London: no pub-
     lisher, 1808. 104p.

48. BANCROFT, Hubert Howe (1832-1918)
     Resources and Development of Mexico. San Fran-
     cisco: A. L. Bancroft and Co., 1893. xiii, 604p.

49. BANDELIER, Adolph Francis Alphonse (1840-1914)
     The Gilded Man: El Dorado. New York: D.
     Appleton and Co., 1893. 302p.

50. BANDELIER, Adolph Francis Alphonse
     Report on an Archaeological Tour in Mexico in

1881. Boston: Cupples, Upham and Co., 1884.
x, 326p.

51. BANDELIER, Adolph Francis Alphonse
A Scientist on the Trail. Travel Letters [1880-81]. Berkeley: The Quivira Society, 1949. vi,
142p. (Reprinted: New York, The Arno Press,
1967.)

52. (BARBOUR, Philip Norbourne) (1813-46)
Journals of the Late Brevet Major ... and his
Wife Isabella Hopkins Barbour. Written During
the War with Mexico... [1846]. New York: G. P.
Putnam's Sons, 1936. 187p. (Edited by R. van
B. T. Doubleday.)

53. "BARD, Samuel A." (pseud. for Ephraim George
Squier, 1821-88)
Waikna; or Adventures on the Mosquito Shore.
New York: Harper and Brothers, 1855. 366p.
(Fiction, but true adventures.) (Reprinted:
Gainesville, University of Florida Press, 1965.)

54. BARCLAY, Alexander
A Practical View of the Present State of Slavery
in the West Indies. London: Smith, Elder and
Co., 1826. xxv, 462p.

55. BARINETTI, Carlo
A Voyage to Mexico and Havana [and the United
States]. New York: G. Vinton, 1841. x, 139p.

56. BARNARD, Major Jonathan C.
The Isthmus of Tehuantepec [inter-ocean railroad
survey]. New York: D. Appleton and Co., 1852.
295p.

57. "A BARRISTER" (pseud. for ------- Forbes)
Trip to Mexico, or Recollections of a ten months
Ramble in 1849-1850. London: Smith, Elder
and Co., 1851. 256p.

58. BARRY, William C. E.
Venezuela [Orinoco and Guianas in 1886]. London:
Marshall, 1886. lxxviii, 159p.

59. BARSKETT, Sir James (or Basket)
     A History of the Island of St. Domingo [and
     description]. London: A. Constable and Co.,
     1818. xiv, 446p. (Reprint: Westport, Negro
     Universities Press, 1971, 1924 edition, viii, 266p.)

60. BARTLETT, John Russell (1805-86)
     Personal Narrative of Explorations and Incidents
     [in Southwest United States; Sonora and Chihuahua,
     Mexico, 1850-53]. New York: Appleton, 1854.
     2 vols. xxii, 506, xvii, 642p. (also London,
     1854.) (Reprint: Chicago, Rio Grande Press,
     1965.)

61. BATES, Henry Walter (1825-92)
     Central America, the West Indies and South
     America. London: John Murray? 1878. 571p.

62. BATES, Henry Walter
     Contributions to an Insect Fauna of the Amazon
     Valley. London: John Murray? 1867. 258p.

63. BATES, Henry Walter
     The Naturalist on the River Amazons, 1848-59.
     London: John Murray, 1863. 2 vols. ix, 351,
     vi, 423p. (Reprinted: Berkeley, University of
     California Press, 1962. one volume. x, 469p.;
     and London, Dent, 1969.)

64. BATES, James Hale (1826-1901)
     Notes of a Tour in Mexico and California. New
     York: Burr Printing House, 1887. viii, 167p.

65. BAXLEY, Dr. Henry Willis (1803-76)
     What I Saw on the West Coast of South and North
     America [Peru, Chile, Hawaii]. New York: D.
     Appleton and Co., 1865. 632p.

66. BAXTER, Sylvester (1850-1927)
     The Cruise of a Land-Yacht [Mexico]. Boston:
     The Authors' Mutual Publishing Co., 1891. iv,
     263p.

67. BAYLEY, Frederic William Naylor (1808-53)
     Four Years' Residence in the West Indies [1826-
     29]. London: W. Kidd, 1830. viii, 693p. (En-
     larged edition, London, 1833. xiii, 742p.)

68. BAZ, Gustavo Adolfo (1852-1904) and E. L. Gallo
History of the Mexican Railway. Wealth of Mexico in the Region Extending from the Gulf to the
Capital. Mexico: Gallo, 1876. 211p. (translated from Spanish.)

69. BEALE, Thomas
The Natural History of the Sperm Whale... [Peru,
Patagonia, South Seas, etc.]. London: John Van
Voorst, 1839. 405p. second edition.

70. BEARD, Rev. John R. (1800-76)
The Life of Toussaint L'Ouverture... [history and
description of Haiti]. London: Ingram, Cooke
and Co., 1853. xiv, 335p. (Reprinted: Westport,
Negro Universities Press, 1970; Freeport, Books
for Libraries, 1971.)

71. BEAUFOY, Mark (1764-1827)
Mexican Illustrations, Founded upon Facts. London: Carpenter and Son, 1828. xii, 310p.

72. BEAUMONT, J. A. B.
Travels in Buenos Aires and the Adjacent Prov-
inces of the Rio de la Plata [1826]. London:
James Ridgway, 1828. xii, 270p.

73. BEAUREGARD, Pierre Gustave Toutant (1818-93)
With Beauregard in Mexico. The Mexican War
Reminiscences of... [March to Sept. 1847].
Baton Rouge: Louisiana State University Press,
1956 (first edition). 115p. (Reprinted: New
York, Da Capo Press, 1969.)

74. BECHER, Henry C. R.
A Trip to Mexico: a Journey from Lake Erie
to Lake Tezcuco and Back. Toronto: Willing
and Williamson, 1880. xiii, 183p.

75. BEERBOHM, Julian (1854-1906)
Wanderings in Patagonia, or Life Among the
Ostrich-Hunters [1877-79?]. New York: Henry
Holt and Co., 1879. 278p. ("New Edition,"
London: Chatto and Windus, 1881. 256p.)

76. BELCHER, Capt. Sir Edward (1799-1877)
The Narrative of a Voyage around the World of

H. M. S. Sulphur [Ecuador, Colombia, Panama, etc.,
1836-42]. London: H. Colburn, 1843, 2 vols.,
with Atlas of 60 plates.

77. BELL, Charles Napier (b. 1854)
Tangweera; Life and Adventures Among Gentle
Savages [Mosquito Indians, British Honduras].
London: Richard Arnold, 1899. xi, 318p.

78. BELL, Sir Henry Hesketh Joudou (1864-1952)
Obeah. Witchcraft in the West Indies. London:
S. Low, Marston, Searle and Rivington, 1899.
viii, 200p. (Reprinted: Westport, Negro Universities Press, 1970.)

79. BELL, Thomas W. (1815-71)
A Narrative of the Capture and Subsequent Sufferings of the Mier Prisoners in Mexico. De
Sota Co., Miss.: R. Morris and Co., 1845.
108p. (Reprinted: Waco, Texan Press, 1964.)

80. BELT, Thomas (1832-78)
The Naturalist in Nicaragua; the Old Mines of
Chontales.... London: J. Murray, 1874. xvi,
403p.

81. BENJAMIN, Samuel Green Wheeler (1837-1914)
The Atlantic Islands as Resorts of Health and
Pleasure [Bahamas, Bermuda, etc.]. New York:
Harper and Brothers, 1878. 274p.

82. BENNETT, Frank
Forty Years in Brazil [ca. 1875 and after].
London: Mills and Boon, 1914. xxiv, 271p.

83. BENNETT, George Washington
An Illustrated History of British Guiana [and
description]. Georgetown: Richardson and Co.,
1866. xviii, 265p. (new title: A History of
British Guiana, 1873, viii, 127p.)

84. BENTHAM, George (1800-84) (sometimes listed under
R. B. Hines)
The Botany of the Voyage of H. M. S. Sulphur
[North America and Latin America]. London:
Smith, Elder and Co., 1844. 410p. (Reprinted:
New York, Stechert-Hafner, 1968.)

85. BERNAU, Rev. John Henry
 Missionary Labours in British Guiana... [manners,
 customs, etc.]. London: J.F. Shaw, 1847. xi,
 242p.

86. BIART, Lucian (1828-97)
 Adventures of a Young Naturalist [Mexico, 1864-].
 New York: Harper and Brothers, 1871. 491p.
 (Edited and adapted by Parker Gilmore.)

87. BIART, Lucian
 My Rambles in the New World [Cuba, Mexico,
 United States and Canada]. London: S. Low,
 Marston, Searle and Revington, 1877. xi, 300p.
 (translated from French.)

88. BICKELL, Rev. R.
 The West Indies as they are [slavery, chiefly in
 Jamaica]. London: J. Hatchard and Son, and
 Lupton Relfe, 1825. xvi, 256p.

89. BIDWELL, Charles Toll (d. 1887)
 The Isthmus of Panama. London: Chapman and
 Hall, 1865. 418p.

90. BIGELOW, John (1817-1911)
 Jamaica in 1850, or the Effects of Sixteen Years
 of Freedom on the Slave Colony. New York:
 George P. Putnam, 1851. iv, 214p. (Reprinted:
 Westport, Negro Universities Press, 1970.)

91. BIGELOW, John (b. 1854)
 Reminiscences of the Santiago Campaign [Cuba;
 description]. New York: Harper, 1899. 187p.

92. BIGELOW, John
 Wit and Wisdom of the Haitians. New York:
 Scribner and Armstrong, 1877. 112p.

93. BIGG-WITHER, Thomas Plantagenet (1845-90)
 Pioneering in South Brazil... [in Province of
 Paraná]. London: John Murray, 1878. 2 vols.
 xvi, 378, xii, 328p. (Reprinted: New York,
 Greenwood Press, 1968.)

94. (BIGGS, James)
 The History of Don Francisco de Miranda's

Attempt to Effect a Revolution in South America...
[letters to a friend in the United States]. Boston:
Oliver and Munroe, 1808. xv, 312p.

95. BINGLEY, Rev. William (1774-1823) (editor)
     Travels in South America. From Modern Writers
     ... [for "young persons"]. London: J. Sharpe,
     1820. 346p.

96. BIRD, Mark Baker (1807-1880)
     The Republic of Hayti and its Struggles. London:
     Elliot Stock, 1867. 461p. (new title: The Black
     Man or Haytian Independence, New York: The
     Author, 1869.)

97. BISHOP, Nathaniel Holmes (1837-1902)
     The Pampas and Andes. A Thousand Miles' Walk
     Across South America [Argentina, Chile, 1854-5].
     Boston: Lee and Shepard, 1868. 310p.

98. BISHOP, William Henry (1847-1928)
     Old Mexico and Her Lost Provinces. A Journey
     in Mexico, Southern California and Arizona by way
     of Cuba. [1881-]. New York: Harper and
     Brothers, 1883. xii, 509p.

99. BLAKE, Mary Elizabeth McGrath (1840-1907) and
     Margaret F. Sullivan
     Mexico. Picturesque--Political--Progressive.
     Boston: Lee and Shepard, 1888. 228p.

100. BLAND, Theodorick
      Report on South America [Chile]. Washington:
      Government Printing Office, 1818. 147p.

101. BLANEY, Henry Robertson (b. 1855)
      The Golden Caribbean [Central America and
      Colombia at end of century]. Boston: Lee and
      Shepard, 1900. viii, 117p.

102. BLEBY, Henry
      Death Struggles of Slavery [Jamaica by 17 years
      resident missionary]. London: Hamilton, Adams
      and Co., 1853. iv, 304p.

103. BLEBY, Henry
      Scenes in the Caribbean Sea. London: Hamilton,
      1854. 210p.

104. BLOOMFIELD, J. H.
     A Cuban Expedition. London: Downey and Co.,
     1898. xi, 296p.

105. BLUNT, Edmund March (1770-1862)
     The American Coast Pilot, Containing Directions
     for the Principal Harbours, Capes and Highlands
     of the Coasts of North and South America. New
     York: E. and G. W. Blunt, 1827. xvi, 674p.
     (11th edition.)

106. BODDAM-WHETHAM, John (b. 1843)
     Across Central America [Guatemala]. London:
     Hurst and Blackett, 1877. xii, 353p.

107. BODDAM-WHETHAM, John
     Roraima and British Guiana [myths, etc.].
     London: Hurst and Blackett, 1879. xx, 363p.

108. BOLINGBROKE, Henry (1785-1855)
     A Voyage to the Demerary and an Account of the
     Settlements There... [Guianas]. London: R.
     Phillips, 1807. 400p.

109. BOLLAERT, William (1807-76)
     Antiquarian, Ethnological and other Researches
     in New Granada, Ecuador, Peru and Chile [in
     1850s]. London: Trübner and Co., 1860. 279p.

110. BONSEL, Stephen (1865-1951)
     The Real Condition of Cuba Today. New York:
     Harper, 1897. viii, 156p.

111. BOUCARD, Adolph
     Travels of a Naturalist. A Record of Adventures,
     Discoveries, History and Customs of the Ameri-
     can Indians [and animals of North and South
     America]. London: Pardy and Son, 1894.
     viii, 204p.

112. BOURGADE La Dardye, Dr. Emmanuel de (b. 1854)
     Paraguay: The Land and People, Natural Wealth
     and Commercial Capabilities. London: George
     Philip and Sons, 1892. xiv, 243p. (translated
     from the French.)

113. BOURNE, Capt. Benjamin Franklin
      The Captive in Patagonia... [1849-   ].   Boston:
      Gould and Lincoln, 1853.   233p.

114. BOURNE, Simon A. B.
      Observations upon the Mexican Province of Texas.
      London: William and Samuel Graves, 1828.   ?p.

115. BOWERS, Lt. William
      Naval Adventures During 35 Years' Service [Chile
      and Peru, San Martín, O'Higgins].   London:
      Richard Bentley, 1833.   2 vols.   xv, 302, xi,
      302p.

116. BOX, Capt. Michael James
      Captain James Box's Adventures and Explorations
      in New and Old Mexico [ten years in North
      Mexico and Arizona].   New York: Derby and
      Jackson, 1861.   344p.

117. BOYD, Robert Nelson (editor)
      Chili.   Sketches of Chili and the Chilians during
      the War 1879-80.   London: W. H. Allan and Co.,
      1881.   vii, 235p.

118. BOYLE, Frederick (b. 1841)
      A Ride Across a Continent [Central America,
      Nicaragua, Costa Rica].   London: Richard
      Bentley, 1868.   2 vols.   xxviii, 299, viii, 297p.

119. BRACKENRIDGE, Henry Marie (1766-1871)
      Voyage to Buenos Aires Performed in the Years
      1817 and 1818.   Baltimore: The Author, 1819.
      2 volumes.   351, 381p.   (Reprinted: New York,
      A. M. S. Press, 1971.)

120. BRACKETT, Albert Gallatin (1829-96)
      General Lane's Brigade in Central Mexico [his-
      tory and description].   Cincinnati: H. W. Derby
      and Co., 1854.   336p.

121. BRAND, Lt. Charles
      Journal of a Voyage to Peru... [and Chile and
      Buenos Aires].   London: H. Colburn, 1828.
      346p.

122. BRASSEY, Mrs. Annie Allnutt (Baroness) (1839-87)
      In the Trades, the Tropics and the Roaring
      Forties [West Indies, etc.]. London: Long-
      mans, Green, 1885.   xiv, 532p.

123. BRASSEY, Annie (Allnutt)
      A Voyage in the "Sunbeam" [Chile, Argentina,
      and Brazil]. London: Longmans, Green, 1878.
      519p.

124. BREEN, Henry Hegart (1805-1888)
      St. Lucia: Historical, Statistical and Descriptive.
      London: Longman, Brown, Green and Longmans,
      1844. xi, 423p.

125. BREMER, Fredrika (1801-65)
      The Homes of the New World.   Impressions of
      America [including Cuba, 1848-]. London:
      A. Hall, 1853. 3 volumes; New York: Harper
      and Brothers, 1853, 2 volumes. (Reprinted:
      Westport, Negro Universities Press, 1971.   2
      volumes.)

126. BRETT, Rev. William Henry (1818-86)
      Indian Missions in Guiana. London: G. Bell,
      1851. ix, 301p.

127. BRETT, Rev. William Henry
      The Indian Tribes of Guiana; their Condition and
      Habits. London: Bell and Daldy, 1851. xiii,
      500p.

128. BRETT, Rev. William Henry (editor)
      Legends and Myths of the Aboriginal Indians of
      British Guiana [prose and poetry]. London:
      W. W. Gardner, 1880. 206p.

129. BRETT, Rev. William Henry
      Mission Work Among the Indian Tribes in the
      Forests of Guiana. London: Society for Pro-
      moting Christian Knowledge, 1881. xii, 260p.;
      and New York: E. and J.B. Young, 1881.

130. BRIDGES, Rev. George Wilson
      The Annals of Jamaica. London: J. Murray,
      1827-28. 2 volumes. xix, 604, xii, 506p.

(Reprinted: Westport, Negro Universities Press, 1971. 2 volumes.)

131. BRIGGS, Lloyd Vernon (b. 1863)
     Arizona and New Mexico [and Mexico and Cali-
     fornia, 1891]. Boston: Privately Printed, 1932.
     x, 285p.

132. BRIGGS, Lloyd Vernon
     Experiences of a Medical Student in Honolulu and
     the Island of Cuba, 1881. Boston: Donald D.
     Nickerson, 1926. xii, 251p.

133. BRIGHAM, William Tufts (1841-1926)
     Guatemala; the Land of the Quetzal. New York:
     Charles Scribner's Sons, 1887. xvi, 453p. (Re-
     printed: Gainesville, University of Florida Press,
     1965.)

134. BRINE, Vice Admiral Lindesay (1834-1906)
     Travels Amongst American Indians... [Mexico,
     Yucatan, Guatemala]. London: S. Low, Marston
     and Co., 1894. xvi, 429p.

135. BRINTON, Daniel Garrison (1837-99) (editor)
     Myths of the New World... [Indian symbolism and
     mythology]. New York: Leypoldt and Holt, 1868.
     viii, 307p. (Reprinted: New York, Greenwood,
     1969.)

136. BROCKLEHURST, Thomas Unett
     Mexico To-Day: A Country with a Great Future
     [includes antiquities]. London: John Murray,
     1883. xvi, 259p.

137. BROMLEY, Mrs. Clara Fitzroy (Kelly)
     A Woman's Wanderings in the Western World. A
     Series of Letters Addressed to Sir Fitzroy Kelly
     by his Daughter [Mexico, West Indies, South
     America, United States and Canada]. London:
     Saunders and Otley, 1861. 299p.

138. BRONKHURST, Rev. H. V. P. (1836-95)
     Among the Hindus and Creoles of British Guiana.
     London: T. Woolmer, 1888. xi, 307p.

139. BRONKHURST, Rev. H. V. P.
     The Colony of British Guiana and its Labouring
     Population. London: T. Woolmer, 1883. xii,
     479p.

140. BROOKS, Nathan C.
     A Complete History of the Mexican War... [de-
     scriptions of military and naval operations, etc.].
     Philadelphia: Gregg, 1849. 558p.

141. BROOME, Henry Arthur (b. 1857)
     The Log of the Rolling Stone [Brazil, Chile, Andes].
     London: T. Werner Laurie, 1857. xv, 325p.

142. BROWN, C.
     A Narrative of the Expedition to South America
     which Sailed from England at the Close of 1817
     for the Service of the Spanish Patriots.... Lon-
     don: John Booth, 1819. 194p.

143. BROWN, Charles Barrington
     Canoe and Camp Trip in British Guiana. London:
     E. Stanford, 1876. 400p.

144. BROWN, Charles Barrington and William Lidstone
     Fifteen Thousand Miles on the Amazon and its
     Tributaries [1873-4]. London: Edward Stanford,
     1878. xvi, 520p.

145. BROWN, Charles Barrington and J. G. Sawkins
     Reports of the Physical, Descriptive and Economic
     Geology of British Guiana. London: H. M. Sta-
     tionary Office, 1875. 297p.

146. BROWN, Capt. Charles H.
     Insurrection at Magellan [his imprisonment in
     Chile]. Boston: George E. Rand, 1854. 228p.

147. BROWN, Dr. Jonathan
     History and Present Condition of St. Domingo.
     Philadelphia: W. Marshall, 1837. 2 volumes.
     iv, 307, 289p.

148. BRYAN, William Smith (b. 1846) (editor)
     Our Islands and their People as Seen with Camera
     and Pencil [Cuba and West Indies]. New York:
     N. D. Townsend, 1899-1900. 2 volumes.

149. BRYANT, Joshua
      An Account of an Insurrection of the Negro Slaves
      of the Colony of Demerara [Aug. 1823]. George-
      town: A. Stevenson, 1824. vii, 124p.

150. BRYANT, William Cullen (1794-1878)
      Cuba and the Cubans. New York: D. Appleton,
      1884? 120p.

151. BUCHNER, J. H.
      The Moravians in Jamaica... [history and de-
      scription from 1830, of their mission]. (title
      varies.) London: Longman, 1854. 175p.

152. BUFFUM, Edward Gould (1820-67)
      Six Months in the Gold Mines; from a Journal of
      Three Years Residence in Upper and Lower Cali-
      fornia, 1847-8-9. Philadelphia: Lee and
      Blanchard, 1850. xi, 244p.; London: R. Bent-
      ley, 1850.

153. BUHOUP, Jonathan W.
      Narrative of the Central Division, or Army in
      Chahuahua [Mexico; description of country and
      people]. Pittsburgh: M. P. Morse, 1847. xii,
      168p.

154. BULLARD, Henry Adams (author possibly James
      Biggs)
      A History of Don Francisco de Miranda's Attempt
      to Effect a Revolution in South America. Boston:
      Oliver and Munroe, 1808. xi, 300p. (Reprinted:
      Clifton, N. J. , A. M. Kelley, 1972.)

155. BULLOCK, William
      Six Months Residence and Travels in Mexico.
      London: John Murray, 1824. 272p. (second
      edition, 1825, two volumes.) (Reprinted: Port
      Washington, Kennikat, 1971 [1824 edition].)

156. BULLOCK, William H.
      Across Mexico in 1864-5. London: Macmillan,
      1866. 396p.

157. BURCHELL, William F. (editor)
      Memoir of Thomas Burchell, Twenty-two Years
      a Missionary in Jamaica [1823-46]. London:
      publisher unknown, 1849. 416p.

158. BURKE, Ulick Ralph (1845-95) and Robert Staples, Jr.
     Business and Pleasure in Brazil. New York:
     Scribner and Welford, 1886. iv, 148p. (Also
     London edition, 1886.)

159. BURNLEY, William Hardin
     Observations of the Present Condition of the Is-
     land of Trinidad. London: Longman, 1842.
     177p.

160. BURTON, Sir Richard Francis (1821-90)
     Explorations of the Highlands of Brazil, with a
     full Account of the Gold and Diamond Mines. Also
     Canoeing down 1500 Miles of the Great River São
     Francisco from Sabará to the Sea. London:
     Tinsley Brothers, 1869. 2 volumes. xii, 443,
     viii, 478p. (Reprinted: New York, Greenwood,
     1969.)

161. BURTON, Capt. Richard Francis
     Letters from the Battle-Fields of Paraguay. Lon-
     don: Tinsley Brothers, 1870. xx, 491p.

162. BUTLER, Frank Hedges (1855-1928)
     Fifty Years of Travel by Land, Water and Air
     [Venezuela, Guiana in late 19th and early 20th
     centuries]. London: T. F. Unwin, 1920. 421p.

163. BUTLER, Rev. John Wesley (1851-1918)
     Sketches of Mexico [prehistoric, colonial, etc.].
     New York: Hunt and Eaton, 1894. x, 316p.;
     also Cincinnati: Cranston and Curts, 1894.

164. BUTLER, William (1818-99)
     Mexico in Transition, from the Power of Political
     Romanism to Civil and Religious Liberty [history
     and description]. New York: Hunt and Eaton,
     1892, 324p.; also Cincinnati: Cranston and Curts,
     1892.

165. BUTTERFIELD, Carlos
     United States and Mexican Mail Steamship Line
     and Statistics of Mexico. New York: J. A. H.
     Hasbrouck and Co., 1859. 109p.

166. BUTTERFIELD, Carlos
     United States and Mexico. Commerce, Trade and

Postal Facilities between the Two Countries....
New York: J. A. H. Hasbrouck and Co. , 1861.
188p.

167. BUTTERWORTH, Hezekiah (1839-1905)
In the Land of the Condor.   A Story of Tarapacá.
Philadelphia: Baptist Travel and Book Society,
1898.   192p.

168. BUTTERWORTH, Hezekiah
Lost in Nicaragua....   Boston: W. A. Wilde and
Co. , 1898.   294p.

169. BUTTERWORTH, Hezekiah
Over the Andes.   Our Boys in New South America.
Boston: W. A. Wilde and Co. , 1897.   370p.

170. BUTTERWORTH, Hezekiah
South America... [and Cuba; history and descrip-
tion].   New York: Doubleday and McClure Co. ,
1898.   xxii, 264p.

171. BUTTERWORTH, Hezekiah (editor)
Traveler Tales of the Pan American Countries
[19th century].   Boston: Dana, Estes and Co. ,
1902.   viii, 289p.   (Reprinted: New York,
A. M. S. Press, 1971.)

172. BUXTON, George Frederick Augustus
Adventures in Mexico and the Rocky Mountains.
London: John Murray, 1847.   ?p.

173. BYAM, George
Wanderings in Some of the Western Republics
of South America [six years in 1830s and 1840s;
Chile, etc.].   London: John W. Parker, 1850.
xii, 264p.

174. BYAM, George
Wild Life in the Interior of Central America.
London: John W. Parker, 1849.   viii, 253p.

C

175. CABRERA, Raimundo (1852-1923)
Cuba and the Cubans.   Philadelphia: Levytipe

Co., 1896. 442p. (translated from Spanish.)

176. CADMAN, John (1814-1900)
     Ten Months in Brazil. Boston: Lee and Shepard,
     1867. ?p.

177. CALDCLEUGH, Alexander (d. 1858)
     Travels in South America, During the Years 1819,
     1820, 1821 [Argentina, Chile, Brazil]. London:
     John Murray, 1825. 2 volumes. xii, 373, viii,
     380p.

178. CALDECOTT, Alfred (1850-1936)
     The Church in the West Indies. New York: E.
     and J. B. Young, 1898. viii, 275p. (Reprinted:
     London, Frank Cass, 1970.)

179. CALDERON, Clímaco and Edward E. Britton
     Colombia, 1893. New York: Robert Sneider,
     1894. 122p.

180. CALDERON de la Barca, Mrs. Francis Erskine
     Ingles (1804-82)
          Life in Mexico During a Residence of two Years
          in that Country [1839-42]. London: Chapman and
          Hall, 1843. xxxviii, 542p. (Reprinted: Garden
          City, Doubleday and Co., 1970. xxx, 834p.)

181. CALVO, Joaquín Bernardo (1857-1915)
     The Republic of Costa Rica [history and descrip-
     tion]. Chicago: Rand-McNally and Co., 1890.
     202p.

182. CAMPBELL, Reau
     Campbell's New Revised Complete Guide and
     Descriptive Book of Mexico. Chicago: Poole
     Brothers, 1859. 256p.

183. CAMPBELL, Reau
     Mexico and the Mexicans. Mexico: Sonora News
     Co., 1892. 131p.

184. CAMPBELL, W. O.
     Through Patagonia [end of century]. London:
     Bickers, 1901. viii, 96p.

185. CANDLER, John (1787-1869)
      Brief Notices of Hayti; with its Condition, Re-
      sources and Prospects. London: T. Ward, 1842.
      viii, 175p.

186. CANDLER, John
      West Indies. Extracts from the Journal of...
      [Jamaica, etc.]. London: Harvey and Darton,
      1840-1. 2 volumes.

187. CANINI, Italo Emileo
      Four Centuries of Spanish Rule in Cuba [history
      and description]. Chicago: Laird and Lee, 1898.
      220p.

188. CAPADOSE, Lt. Col. Henry
      Sixteen Years in the West Indies. London: T. C.
      Newby, 1845. 2 volumes.

189. CARBUTT, Mary (Rhodes) (Mrs. E. H. Carbutt)
      Five Months' Fine Weather in Canada, Western
      United States and Mexico. London: S. Low,
      Marston, Searle and Rivington, 1889. 243p.

190. CAREY, Henry Charles (1793-1879) and J. Lea
      Geography, History and Statistics of America
      and the West Indies. London: Sherwood, Jones
      and Co., 1823. vi, 472p.

191. CARLETON, George Washington
      Our Artist in Cuba, Peru, Spain and Algiers.
      New York: G. W. Carleton and Co., 1877. 144p.

192. CARLETON, James Henry (1814-73)
      The Battle of Buena Vista [description and obser-
      vations]. New York: Harper, 1848. vii, 238p.

193. CARLISLE, Arthur Drummond
      Round the World in 1870 [including South America].
      London: Henry S. King, 1872. xii, 408p.

194. CARMICHAEL, Mrs. Alison
      Domestic Manners and Social Conditions of the
      White, Coloured, and Negro Population of the
      West Indies [1820-25]. London: Whittaker,
      Treacher and Co., 1833. 2 volumes. viii, 336,
      iv, 338p. (Reprinted: New York, Negro Univer-

sities Press, 1969. 2 volumes.)

195.   CARNEGIE-WILLIAMS, Rosa
       A Year in the Andes, or a Lady's Adventures in
       Bogotá [and Panama, Jamaica, Haiti, St. Thomas,
       Aug. 2, 1881 to July 27, 1882; a diary]. London:
       London Literary Society, 1883 or 1884. 270p.

196.   CARPENTER, Frank George (1855-1924)
       South America: Social, Industrial, Political [at
       end of century]. New York: W. W. Wilson, 1900.
       vi, 625p. (also Akron, Saalsfield Publishing Co.,
       1900.)

197.   CARPENTER, William W.
       Travels and Adventures in Mexico [2500 miles
       on foot]. New York: Harper and Brothers, 1851.
       xi, 300p.

198.   CARROLL, H. Bailey and J. Villasana Haggard
       (editors)
       Three New Mexico Chronicles [Pedro Bautista
       Pino, 1812; Antonio Barreiro, 1832; and José
       Agustín de Escudero, 1849]. Albuquerque: The
       Quivira Society, 1941. xxxi, 344p. (Reprinted:
       New York, Arno Press, 1967.)

199.   CASE, Alden Buell (1851-1932)
       Thirty Years with the Mexicans, in Peace and
       Revolution [1884-   ]. New York: Fleming H.
       Revell Co., 1917. 285p.

200.   CASTRO, Lorenzo
       The Republic of Mexico in 1882. New York:
       Thompson and Moreau, 1882. iv, 271p.

201.   CATHCART, William (?)
       Jamaica Almanack of the Year 1846. Kingston:
       The Author (?), 1846. 156, +84p.

202.   CATLIN, George (1796-1872)
       Last Rambles Amongst the Indians of the Rocky
       Mountains and the Andes. New York: D. Apple-
       ton, 1867. x, 361p.

203.   CHALMERS, Col. George (1742-1825)
       Remarks on the Late War in St. Domingo... [and

Jamaica]. London: Rivington, 1803. 115p.

204. CHALONER, Edward
      The Mahogany Tree. Its Botanical Character
      [West Indies, Central America, Mexico]. Liver-
      pool: Rockliff and Son, 1850. 117p.

205. CHAMBERLAIN, Samuel Emery (1829-1908)
      My Confession [soldier in Mexican War]. New
      York: Harper and Brothers, 1856. x, 301p.

206. CHAMPNEY, Mrs. Elizabeth (Williams) (1850-1922)
      Three Vasser Girls in South America. Boston:
      Estes and Lauriat, 1885. x, 239p.

207. CHANDLER, J.
      Brief Notes on Hayti. London: Publisher unknown,
      1842. vi, 175p.

208. CHARLES, Cecil
      Honduras, the Land of Great Depths. Chicago:
      Rand McNally and Co., 1890. 216p.

209. CHARNEY, Claude Joseph Désiré (1828-1915)
      The Ancient Cities of the New World. Being
      Voyages and Explorations in Mexico and Central
      America from 1857-1882. New York: Harper
      and Brothers, 1887. xlvi, 514p. (translation
      from French.)

210. CHESTER, Greville John (1830-92)
      Transatlantic Sketches in the West Indies, South
      America, Canada and the United States. London:
      Smith, Elder and Co., 1869. xvi, 405p.

211. CHESTERTON, General George Laval
      A Narrative of Proceedings in Venezuela, 1819-20.
      London: John and Arthur Arch, 1820. x, 257p.

212. CHEVALIER, M. Michel (1806-79)
      Mexico. Ancient and Modern [history and descrip-
      tion]. London: John Maxwell and Co., 1864.
      2 volumes. xvi, 387, ii, 360p.

213. CHILD, Mrs. Lydia Maria (Frances) (1802-80)
      The Right Way, the Safe Way, Proved by Emanci-
      pation in the British West Indies and Elsewhere.

New York: The Author, 1862. 108p. (Reprinted: Westport, Negro Universities Press, 1971.)

214. CHILD, Theodore (1846-92)
      The Spanish-American Republics [history and description]. New York: Harper and Brothers, 1891. xii, 444p.

215. CHRISTIE, William Dougal (1816-74)
      Notes on Brazilian Questions. London: Macmillan, 1865. lxxi, 236p.

216. CHURCH, George Earl (1835-1910) (editor)
      Explorations Made in the Valley and the River Madeira from 1749 to 1868 [Brazil]. London: National Bolivian Navigation Co., 1875. viii, 355p.

217. CHURCH, George Earl
      The Route to Bolivia via the River Amazon [report to Bolivian and Brazilian governments]. London: Waterlow and Sons, 1877. 216p.

218. CHYNOWETH, W. Harris
      The Fall of Maximilian, Late Emperor of Mexico [history and description]. London: The Author, 1872. viii, 277p.

219. CLARK, E. B.
      Twelve Months in Peru [1873-75?]. London: T. Fisher Unwin, 1891. xxiii, 158p.

220. CLARK, Edwin
      A Visit to South America... [Paraguay, Uruguay, Argentina, 1876-77]. London: Dean and Son, 1878. iv, 355p.

221. CLARK, Hamlet (1823?-67)
      Letters Home from Spain, Algeria and Brazil during past Ethnological Rambles. London: J. Van Voorst, 1862. iv, 178p.

222. CLARK, William Jared (1854?-1922)
      Commercial Cuba. A Book for Business Men. New York: Charles Scribner's Sons, 1898. xviii, 514p.

223.   CLARK, William Jared
       Cuba and the Fight for Freedom.   Philadelphia:
       Scribners, 1896.   ?p.

224.   CLARKE, A. B.
       Travels in Mexico and California.   Boston: Wright
       Hasty, 1852.   138p.

225.   CLEMENS, Eliza Jane McCartney
       La Plata Countries of South America [Argentina,
       Uruguay, Paraguay; 1880-].   Philadelphia: J. B.
       Lippincott Co., 1886.   511p.

226.   CLEVELAND, Richard Jeffry (1773-1860)
       Narrative of Voyages and Commercial Enterprises
       [Rio de Janeiro, 1802, 1806].   Cambridge: John
       Owen, 1842.   2 volumes.   xvi, 249, viii, 240p.

227.   CLEVELAND, Richard Jeffry
       Voyages of a Merchant Navigator [Chile, etc.
       1817-].   New York: Leavitt and Allen, 1855.
       ix, 245p.

228.   CLOUD, William F.
       Church and State.   Or Mexican Politics from
       Cortés to Díaz [history, description].   Kansas
       City: Peck and Clark, 1896.   274p.

229.   CLOUGH, R. Stewart
       The Amazons.   A Diary of a Twelve Month's
       Journey.   London: South American Missionary
       Society, 1872 (or 1873).   240p.

230.   CLUSERET, General Gustave Paul (1823-1900)
       Mexico and the Solidarity of Nations [history and
       description].   New York: Blackwell, 1866 (third
       edition).   109p.

231.   COAN, Rev. Titus (1801-82)
       Adventures in Patagonia.   A Missionary's Explor-
       ing Trip [and Falkland Islands, 1833-].   New
       York: Dodd, Mead and Co., 1880.   319p.

232.   COCHRANE, Charles Stuart
       Journal of a Residence and Travels in Colombia
       during the Years 1823 and 1824.   London: Henry

Colburn, 1825. 2 volumes. xv, 524, viii, 515p.
(Reprinted: New York, A. M. S. Press, 1971.)

233. COCHRANE, Elizabeth (pseud: Nellie Bly) (b. 1867)
Six Months in Mexico. New York: J. W. Lovell,
1888. 205p.; another New York edition, 1888.

234. COCHRANE, Thomas Lord (Tenth Earl of Dundonald)
(1775-1869) (often listed: Thomas Dundonald)
The Autobiography of a Seaman [Chile, Peru,
Brazil]. London: R. Bentley, 1860. 2 volumes.

235. COCHRANE, Thomas Lord
Memorandum of Naval Services in the Liberation
of Chile and Peru from Spanish Domination. London: James Ridgway, 1858. xiii, 239p.

236. COCHRANE, Thomas Lord
Narrative of the Services in the Liberation of
Chili, Peru and Brazil by the Earl of Dundonald
[1817-25]. London: James Ridgway, 1859. 2
volumes. xxii, 293, xi, 305p.

237. CODMAN, John (1814-1900)
The Round Trip by way of Panama through California. New York: G. P. Putnam's Sons, 1879.
xiii, 331p.

238. CODMAN, Capt. John
Ten Months in Brazil... [1864]. Boston: Lee
and Shepard, 1867. 208p.

239. COFFIN, Alfred Oscar
Land without Chimneys, or the Byways of Mexico.
Cincinnati: The Editors Publishing Co., 1898.
352p.

240. (COFFIN, J. F.)
Journal of a Residence in Chile by a Young
American During the Revolutionary Scenes, 1817-
1819. Boston: Wells and Lilly, 1825. 237p.

241. COIT, Deniel Wadsworth (1787-1876)
Digging for Gold without a Shovel. The Letters
of ... From Mexico City to San Francisco, 1848-
51. Denver: Lawton Kennedy, 1967. 116p.
(edited by G. P. Hammond.)

242.   COKE, Thomas (1747-1814)
       A History of the West Indies, Containing the Nat-
       ural, Civil, and Ecclesiastical History of Each
       Island. Liverpool: Nattall, Fisher and Dixon,
       1808-1811. 3 volumes. 459, 483, 543p. (Re-
       printed: London, Cass, 1971.)

243.   COLE, George R. Fitzroy
       The Peruvians at Home. London: Kegan Paul
       and Trench, 1884. xix, 277p.

244.   COLEMAN, Ann Raney
       Victorian Lady on the Texas Frontier. Journal
       of... [Mexican Texas, 1832-]. Norman: Uni-
       versity of Oklahoma Press, 1971. xxii, 206p.
       (edited by C. R. King.)

245.   COLERIDGE, Henry Nelson (1798-1843)
       Six Months in the West Indies in 1825. London:
       John Murray, 1826. 332p. (revised: London,
       T. Tegg, 1862.) (Reprinted: Westport, Negro
       Universities Press, 1970.)

246.   COLLENS, James Henry
       A Guide to Trinidad. London: Elliot Stock, 1888.
       vi, 287p. (second edition.)

247.   COLQUHOUN, Archibald Ross (1848-1914)
       The Key of the Pacific. The Nicaragua Canal
       [1895]. New York: Longmans, Green Co., 1898.
       xx, 443p. (first edition 1895?.)

248.   COLTON, Rev. Walter (1797-1851)
       Deck and Port. Incidents of a Cruise to California
       [Rio de Janeiro, Buenos Aires, Valparaiso, Lima,
       1845]. New York: A. S. Barnes, 1850. 408p.;
       also Cincinnati, H. W. Derby and Co., 1850.

249.   CONDER, Josiah (1789-1885) (editor)
       Brazil and Buenos Aires. London: J. Duncan,
       1825. 2 volumes. (From The Modern Traveler.)

250.   CONDER, Josiah (editor)
       Colombia. London: J. Duncan, 1825. iv, 356p.
       (From The Modern Traveler.)

251. CONDER, Josiah (editor)
      Mexico and Guatemala. London: J. Duncan, 1825.
      2 volumes. (From The Modern Traveler.)

252. CONDER, Josiah (editor)
      Peru and Chile. London: J. Duncan, 1829.
      360p. (From The Modern Traveler.)

253. CONEY, A. K. and José F. Godoy (editors)
      The Legal and Mercantile Handbook of Mexico.
      Chicago: Pan American, 1892. 546p.

254. CONKLING, Alfred Ronald (1850-1917)
      Appleton's Guide to Mexico [and Guatemala].
      New York: D. Appleton and Co., 1883. xvi,
      378p.

255. CONKLING, Howard
      Mexico and the Mexicans, or Notes of Travel in
      the Winter and Spring of 1883. New York: Tainter
      Brothers, 1883. x, 298p.

256. CONWAY, Sir William Martin (1856-1937)
      Aconcagua and Tierra del Fuego. A Book of
      Climbing, Travel and Exploration [1888-1900].
      New York: Cassell and Co., 1902. xii, 252p.

257. CONWAY, Sir William Martin
      The Bolivian Andes [1898-1900]. New York:
      Harper and Brothers, 1901. x, 403p.

258. COOKE, Philip St. George (1809-95)
      Scenes and Adventures in the Army... [Mexican
      War; description of Mexico and the people].
      Philadelphia: Lindsay and Blakeston, 1857. xii,
      432p.

259. COPPINGER, Richard William
      Cruise of the "Alert": Four Years in Patagonia,
      Polynesian and Mascerne Waters, 1878-82. Lon-
      don: W. Swan Sonnenschein, 1883. xiii, 256p.

260. CORY, Charles Barney (1857-1921)
      The Birds of the Bahama Islands. Boston: The
      Author, 1880. 250p.

261.   COULTER, Dr. John
        Adventures in the Pacific... [lands, peoples, mis-
        sionaries; Chile]. Dublin: William Curry, Jr.
        1845. xi, 290p.

262.   COULTER, Dr. John
        Adventures on the Western Coasts of South Amer-
        ica [and Pacific islands and California]. London:
        Longman, Brown, Green and Longmans, 1847. 2
        volumes. xxiv, 288, xii, 278p.

263.   COURTNEY, William S.
        The Gold Fields of Santo Domingo. New York:
        Anson P. Norton, 1860. 144p.

264.   COUTS, Cave Johnson (1821-74)
        Hepah, California. The Journal of ... From
        Monterey, Nueva Leon, Mexico to Los Angeles,
        California during the Years 1848-49. Tucson:
        Arizona Pioneer Historical Society, 1961. 113p.
        (edited by Henry F. Dobyns.)

265.   COX, Guillermo Eloi
        Expedition Across the Southern Andes of Chile
        [and Patagonia]. Santiago: The Author, 1864.
        viii, 273p. (tr. from Spanish.)

266.   CRAIG, Neville B. (1847-1926)
        Recollections of an Ill-Fated Expedition to the
        Headwaters of the Madeira in Brazil [1878-79].
        Philadelphia: J.B. Lippincott, 1907. 479p.

267.   CRAWFORD, Cora Hayward
        The Land of the Montezumas. New York: John
        B. Alden, 1889. xiv, 311p.

268.   CRAWFORD, Robert
        Across the Pampas and the Andes [Argentina,
        Chile, 1871-]. London: Longmans, Green and
        Co., 1884. xxii, 344p.

269.   CRAWFORD, Robert
        South American Sketches [Uruguay, etc., 1888-92].
        London: Longmans, Green and Co., 1898. xx,
        280p.

270. CROMMELIN, Maria Henrietta de la Cherois
Over the Andes, from the Argentine to Chile and
Peru. London: Richard Bentley, 1896. viii,
387p.

271. CROSBY, Elisha Oscar
Memoirs of ... Reminiscences of California and
Guatemala from 1848-1864. San Marino: Hunting-
ton Library, 1945. xxvi, 119p. (edited by C. A.
Barker.)

272. CROWE, Frederick
The Gospel in Central America. London: Charles
Gilpin, 1850. xii, 588p.

273. CULBERTSON, Rosamond
Rosamund Culbertson; or a Narrative of the Cap-
tivity and Sufferings of an American Female under
the Popish Priests in the Island of Cuba.... London: J. S. Hodson, 1837. viii, 144p.

274. CUNDALL, Frank (1858-1937) and F. S. A. (editors)
Lady Nugent's Journal. Jamaica 100 Years Ago
[1801-1815]. London: A. and C. Black, 1907.
404p.

275. CUNNINGHAM, Robert Oliver (d. 1918)
Notes on the Natural History of the Strait of
Magellan and West Coast of Patagonia [and Rio
de Janeiro, 1866-69]. Edinburgh: Edmonston
and Douglas, 1871. xvi, 517p.

276. CURTIS, William Eleroy (1850-1911)
Between the Andes and the Ocean. An Account of
an Interesting Journey Down the West Coast of
South America from the Isthmus of Panama to the
Straits of Magellan. Chicago: Stone and Co.,
1900. vi, 442p.

277. CURTIS, William Eleroy
The Capitals of Spanish America. New York:
Harper and Brothers, 1888. xvi, 715p. (Re-
printed: New York, Praeger, 1969.)

278. CURTIS, William Eleroy
Venezuela, Land Where it's Always Summer. New
York: Harper and Brothers, 1896. vi, 315p.

279.   CUSHING, Sumner Webster (b. 1818)
       Wild Oats Sowings [with Garibaldi in Argentina].
       New York: D. Fanshaw, 1857. 483p.

                              D

280.   DAHLGREN, Charles Bunker
       Historic Mines of Mexico; a Review of the Mines
       of that Republic for the Past Three Centuries
       [based on Von Humboldt, Ward, Burkgart...].
       New York: The Author, 1883. 220p.

281.   DAHLGREN, Madeleine Vinton (1835-98)
       South Sea Sketches. A Narrative [Peru, Chile].
       Boston: James R. Osgood, 1881. 238p.

282.   DALLAS, Robert Charles (1754-1824)
       The History of the Maroons [Jamaica slaves; and
       Cuba]. London: T. N. Longman and O. Rees,
       1803. 2 volumes. xii, cxiv, 359, xi, 514p.
       (Reprinted: London, Frank Cass, 1971?.)

283.   DALTON, Henry G.
       The History of British Guiana, Comprising a
       General Description of the Colony... [by a Creole
       Doctor]. London: Longman, Brown, Green and
       Longmans, 1855. 2 volumes. xvi, 518, vii, 580p.

284.   DANA, Richard Henry (1815-82)
       To Cuba and Back. A Vacation Voyage. Boston:
       Ticknor and Fields, 1859. 288p. (London edition
       in same year.) (Reprinted: Carbondale, Univer-
       sity of Southern Illinois, 1966.)

285.   DANCE, Charles Daniel
       Recollections of Four Years in Venezuela. Lon-
       don: Henry S. King, 1876. xii, 303p.

286.   DANCER, Dr. Thomas
       The Medical Assistant, or Jamaica Practice of
       Physic.... Jamaica: Alex Aikman, 1819 (third
       edition). viii, 355p.

287.   DARBYSHIRE, Charles
       My Life in the Argentine Republic [1852; 1893-4].

New York: Frederick Warne, 1918. xii, 140p.
(also a London edition, 1918.)

288. DARWIN, Charles Robert (1809-82)
      Geological Observations on South America [voyage
      of Beagle, 1831-36]. London: Smith, Elder and
      Co., 1846. vii, 279p. (other titles and dates.)

289. DARWIN, Charles Robert
      Journal of Researches into the Geology and Natural
      History of the Various Countries Visited by H. M. S.
      Beagle [1831-36; including South America]. London:
      H. Colburn, 1839. viii, 507p. (reprinted with dif-
      ferent titles and dates.)

290. DAUXION-LAVAYSSE, Jean François (1775-1826)
      A Statistical, Commercial and Political Description
      of Venezuela... [and West Indies, 1792-1806].
      London: G. and W. B. Whittaker, 1820. 2 volumes.
      (Translated from French.) (Reprinted: Westport,
      Negro Univ. Press, 1970. 1 vol. xxxix, 479p.

291. DAVENPORT, Bishop
      A New Gazeteer: or, Geographical Dictionary of
      North America and the West Indies. Baltimore:
      M'Dowell, 1832. 471p. (Also Providence: 1832.)
      (Later editions with changed titles, publishers,
      and dates.)

292. DAVEY, Richard Patrick Boyle (b. 1848)
      Cuba, Past and Present. New York: Charles
      Scribner's Sons, 1898. viii, 284p. (Also London:
      Chapman and Hall, 1898.)

293. DAVIE, John Constanse
      Letters from Buenos Aires and Chile [1804-1813].
      London: R. Aikerman, 1819. xi, 323p.

294. DAVIE, John Constanse
      Letters from Paraguay ... Written During a Resi-
      dence of Seventeen Months in that Country [Para-
      guay, Uruguay, Argentina]. London: G. Robin-
      son, 1805. vii, 293p.

295. DAVIS, Raymond Cazallis (1836-1919)
      Reminiscences of a Voyage Around the World
      [Maine, via Cape Horn to San Francisco]. Ann Arbor:
      Dr. Chase's Steam Printing House, 1869. 331p.

296.   DAVIS, Richard Harding (1864-1916)
       Cuba in War Time.   New York: R. H. Russell,
       1897.   143p.

297.   DAVIS, Richard Harding
       The Cuban and Puerto Rican Campaigns.   New
       York: Scribner's, 1898.   xiii, 360p.

298.   DAVIS, Richard Harding
       Three Gringos in Venezuela and Central America.
       New York: Harper and Brothers, 1896.   xiv,
       282p.

299.   DAVIS, William Heath (1822-1909)
       Seventy-five Years in California [Mexican and
       United States California, 1831-].   San Fran-
       cisco: J. Howell, 1929.   xxxii, 422p.   (edited
       by Howard A. Small.)   (Reprinted: San Fran-
       cisco, 1967.)

300.   DAVIS, William Heath
       Sixty Years in California [under Mexico and the
       United States].   San Francisco: A. J. Leary,
       1889.   xii, 639p.

301.   DAVY, John (1790-1868)
       The West Indies, Before and Since Slave Emanci-
       pation... [based on a three years' residence].
       London: W. and F. G. Cash, 1854.   viii, 551p.

302.   DAY, Charles William
       Five Years' Residence in the West Indies.   Lon-
       don: Publisher unknown, 1852.   2 volumes.   x,
       335, viii, 318p.

303.   DE BONELLI, L. Hugh
       Travels in Bolivia.   With a Tour Across the
       Pampas to Buenos Aires....   London: Hurst
       and Blackett, 1854.   2 volumes.   315, 328p.

304.   DELAFIELD, John Jr. (1812-1865?)
       An Inquiry into the Origin of the Antiquities of
       America [Appendix on superiority of Northern
       Hemisphere men over Southern, by J. Lakey].
       New York: Colt, Burgess and Co., 1839.   142p.

305. DELANO, Amasa (1763-1823)
      A Narrative of Voyages and Travels in the North-
      ern and Southern Hemispheres... [including Chile
      and Peru]. Boston: E. G. House, 1817. 600p.

306. DELMAR, E. H. (editor)
      Trades Directory and Mercantile Manual of Mexico,
      Central America and the West Indies Islands.
      Chicago and New York: Belford, Clarke and Co.,
      1889-90. 491p.

307. DEL RIO, Capt. Antonio and Paul Félix Cabrera
      Description of the Ruins of an Ancient City [and
      people in Guatemala]. London: Henry Berthoud,
      1822. viii, 128p.

308. DEMING, C.
      Shadows in Cuba. New York: Publisher unknown,
      1884. 124p.

309. DENT, Hastings Charles (b. 1855)
      A Year in Brazil. London: Kegan Paul, Trench
      and Co., 1886. xvii, 444p.

310. DERBY, Edward Henry Stanley (Fifteen Earl of)
      (1826-93)
          Claims and Resources of the West Indian Colonies.
          London: T. and W. Boone, 1850. 111p.

311. DERBY, Edward Henry Stanley
      Further Facts Connected with the West Indies.
      London: T. and W. Boone, 1851. 124p.

312. DERBY, Edward Henry Stanley
      Six Weeks in South America [Colombia, Ecuador,
      Peru]. London: T. and W. Boone, 1850. iv,
      132p.

313. DEWAR, James Cumming
      Voyage of the Nyanza [Argentina, Uruguay, Bolivia,
      Peru, etc., 1887-]. London: William Black-
      wood, 1892. xviii, 446p.

314. DEWELL, James D.
      Down in Porto Rico with a Kodak. New Haven:
      Record Publishing Co., 1898. 102p.

315. DICKINS, Marguerite
      Along Shore with a Man-of-War [east coast of
      South America]. Boston: Arena Publishing Co.,
      1893. 242p.

316. DINGMAN, Benjamin S.
      Ten Years in South America [Peru, Bolivia, Chile,
      Argentina, Uruguay, Brazil]. Montreal: Gazette
      Printing House, 1876. 160p.

317. DINWIDDIE, William (1867-1934)
      Puerto Rico: Its Conditions and Possibilities.
      New York: Harper and Brothers, 1899. vi, 293p.

318. DIXIE, Lady Florence Caroline (1857-1905)
      Across Patagonia [1879]. London: R. Bentley
      and Son, 1880. xvi, 251p.

319. DOMENECH, Emmanuel Henri Dieudonné (1825?-86)
      Missionary Adventures in Texas and Mexico. A
      Personal Narrative of Six Year's Sojourn in these
      Regions. London: Longman, Brown, Green, Long-
      mans and Roberts, 1858. xv, 366p. (tr. from
      French.)

320. DONNAVAN, Corydon
      Adventures in Mexico: Experiences During a Cap-
      tivity of Seven Months. Cincinnati: Robinson and
      Jones, 1847. 132p.

321. DOUBLEDAY, Charles William (b. 1829)
      Reminiscences of the "Filibuster" War in Nic-
      aragua. New York: G. P. Putnam's Sons, 1886.
      ix, 225p.; also London, 1886.

322. DOWNIE, William (b. 1819)
      Adventures in Panama... [and Alaska; hunting
      gold]. San Francisco: The California Publishing
      Co., 1893. 407p.

323. DRAPER, Andrew Sloan (b. 1848)
      The Rescue of Cuba. An Episode in the Growth
      of Free Government. Boston: Silver Burdett,
      1899. 186p.

324. DREES, Charles William
      Thirteen Years in Mexico. From the Letters

of... [Methodist missionary, 1874-87]. New York:
Abingdon Press, 1915. ?p. (edited by Ada M. C.
Dress.)

325. DUANE, William (1760-1835)
      A Visit to Colombia in the Years 1822 and 1823.
      Philadelphia: T. H. Palmer, 1826. 632p.

326. DUCOUDRAY-Holstein, Henri La Fayette Villaume
      (1763-1829)
      Memoirs of Simón Bolívar, President Liberator
      of the Republic of Colombia, and of his Principal
      Generals... [from 1807; history and description].
      Boston: S. G. Goodrich, 1829. 64, +383p.

327. DUFFIELD, Alexander James (1821-90)
      Peru in the Guano Age [1870s]. London: Richard
      Bentley, 1877. 151p.

328. DUFFIELD, Alexander James
      The Prospects of Peru. London: Newman and
      Co., 1881. 120p.

329. DUFFIELD, Alexander James
      Recollections of Travels Abroad [Peru, Bolivia].
      London: Remington, 1889. xiv, 327p.

330. DUGGAN, Janie Prichard
      A Mexican Ranch, or Beauty for Ashes. Chicago:
      Student Missionary Campaign Library, 1891. 377p.
      (semi-fiction.)

331. DUNBAR, Edward Ely (1818-71)
      The Mexican Papers [five papers; reminiscences,
      etc.]. New York: J. A. H. Hasbrouck, 1860.
      279p.

332. DUNBAR, Virginia Lyndall
      A Cuban Amazon [fiction; description]. Cincinnati:
      Editor Publishing Co., 1897. 295p.

333. DUNDAS, Dr. Robert
      Sketches of Brazil [diseases, etc., 1820s through
      1840s]. London: J. Churchill, 1852. x, 449p.

334. DUNLOP, Robert Glasgow
      Travels in Central America [three years, chiefly

in Guatemala]. London: Longman, Brown, Green and Longmans, 1847. viii, 358p.

335. DUNN, Rev. Ballard S.
Brazil the Home for Southerners [after the U.S. Civil War]. New York: G.B. Richardson, 1866. 272p.

336. DUNN, Henry (1800-78)
Guatemala, or the United Provinces of Central America [1827-28]. New York: G. and C. Carvill, 1828. 318p. (different title, London, 1829.)

337. DYOTT, General William (1761-1847)
Dyott's Diary, 1781-1845 [by a British officer; West Indies, etc.]. London: A. Constable and Co., 1907. 2 volumes. (edited by Reginald W. Jeffry.)

E

338. EARDLEY-Wilmot, Sydney Marow (b. 184?)
Our Journal in the Pacific [west coast of South America]. London: Longmans, Green and Co., 1873. xiv, 353p.

339. EASTWICK, Edward Backhouse (1814-83)
Venezuela, or Sketches of Life in a South American Republic [1864]. London: Chapman and Hall, 1865. xii, 418p.

340. EDEN, Charles Henry (1839-1900)
The West Indies. London: S. Low, Marston, Searle and Rivington, 1880. viii, 239p.

341. EDGCUMBE, Edward Robert Pearce (1851-1929)
Ziphyrus. A Holiday in Brazil and on the River Plate. London: Chatto and Windus, 1887. vi, 242p.

342. EDWARD, David Barnett
The History of Texas [descriptive guide under Mexico]. Cincinnati: J.A. James, 1836. 336p.

343. EDWARDS, Charles Lincoln (b. 1863)
Bahama Songs and Stories [folklore]. New York:

Houghton Mifflin, 1895. 111p. (Reprinted: New York, Kraus, 1970.)

344. EDWARDS, William Henry (1822-1909)
Voyage up the River Amazon, Including a Residence in Pará. Philadelphia: Appleton, 1847. 256p. (also New York and London, 1847.)

345. ELTON, James Frederick
With the French in Mexico. London: Chapman and Hall, 1867. x, 206p.

346. ELWES, Robert
A Sketcher's Tour Round the World [Chile, 1849]. London: Hurst and Blackett, 1854. xii, 411p.

347. ELWES, Robert
West, Southwest. A Voyage in that Direction to the West Indies. London: Kerby and Son, 1866. 135p.

348. EMORY, William Hemsley (1811-87)
Report on the United States and Mexican Boundary Survey... [description, North Mexico]. Washington: A.O.P. Nicholson, 1857, 1859. 3 volumes. (34th Cong. 1st Sess. Sen. Ex. Doc. 108.)

349. EMPSON, Charles
Narratives of South America [Colombia]. London: William Edwards, 1836. xvi, 322p.

350. "An English Soldier"
The Mexican War. Comprising Incidents and Adventures in the United States and Mexico with the American Army. New York: Townsend, 1860. 288p.

351. ENGLISH, Henry (1803-55)
A General Guide to the Companies Formed for Working Foreign Mines [South America in the 1820s]. London: Boosey and Sons, 1825. 106p.

352. EQUIANO, Olaudah
The Interesting Narrative of... [impressions of West Indian slavery by a Christian slave]. Halifax: J. Nicholson, 1813. 514p.

353. EVANS, Col. Albert S.
      Our Sister Republic. A Gala Trip Through
      Tropical Mexico in 1869-70.... Toledo: W. E.
      Bliss, 1870. 518p.

354. EVANS, Patrick Fleming
      From Peru to the Plate, Overland [via Bolivia].
      London: Bates and Hendy, 1889. 124p.

355. EVERETT, Alexander H. (pseud: "A Citizen of the
      West")
      America: or a General Survey of the Political
      Situation of the Several Powers of the Western
      Continent. Philadelphia: H. C. Carey and J.
      Lea, 1827. 364p. (Reprinted: New York,
      Kelley, 1971.)

356. EVES, Charles Washington
      The West Indies. London: S. Low, Marston,
      Searle and Rivington, 1889. xxiv, 322p.

357. EWBANK, Thomas (1792-1870)
      Life in Brazil, or a Journal of a Visit to the Land
      of the Cocoa and Palm [1845]. New York: Harper
      and Brothers, 1856. 469p. (Reprinted: Detroit,
      Blaine Ethridge, 1971.)

                              F

358. (FABENS, Joseph Warren) (1821-75)
      In the Tropics, by a settler in Santo Domingo
      [fiction but true adventure]. New York: G. W.
      Carleton, 1863. 306p.

359. (FABENS, Joseph Warren)
      Life in Santo Domingo by a Settler. New York:
      G. W. Carleton, 1873. 308p.

360. FABENS, Joseph Warren
      A Story of Life on the Isthmus [Panama]. New
      York: G. P. Putnam Co., 1853. 215p.

361. FARRER, Thomas (editor)
      Notes on the History of the Church in Guiana.
      Berbice: Gazette Office, 1892. 226p.

362.   (FERGUSON, Arthur W. ?)
       Ferguson's Anecdotal Guide to Mexico, with a
       Map of Railways. Historical, Geological, Archaeo-
       logical and Critical. Philadelphia: Claxton, Tem-
       sen, and Haffelflinger, 1876.   ?p.

363.   (FERGUSON, Arthur W.)
       Mexico; A Handbook.   Washington: Bureau of
       American Republics, 1890.   347p.

364.   FERNAU, E. C.
       The Reign of Rosas, or South American Sketches.
       London: S. Tinsley, 1877. vi, 372p.

365.   FERNEYHOUGH, Thomas
       Military Memoirs of Four Brothers... [British in
       La Plata, 1806-7; and Africa]. London: William
       Sams, 1829. xi, 275p. (enlarged edition: Lon-
       don, Joseph Masters, 1838. xi, 324p.)

366.   FERRY, Gabriel (pseud. for Louis de Bellamare)
       Vagabond Life in Mexico. London: J. Black-
       wood, 1856.   450p.

367.   FEURTADO, Walter Augustus
       The Jubilee Reign of Her Most Gracious Majesty
       Queen Victoria in Jamaica [1837-87]. Jamaica:
       The Author, 1890. vi, 218p.

368.   FINDLEY, Alexander George (1812-75)
       A Directory for the Navigation of the Pacific Ocean;
       with Description of the Coasts, Islands, etc. from
       the Strait of Magellan to the Arctic Sea [South and
       North America]. London: R. H. Laurie, 1851.
       2 volumes. 1472p.

369.   FINDLEY, Alexander George
       A Sailing Directory for the Caribbean, or West
       Indian Islands, from Trinidad to Porto Rico.
       London: R. H. Laurie, 1879. 142p.

370.   FINDLEY, Alexander George
       A Sailing Directory for the Coasts of Brazil,
       from the River Pará to the Río de la Plata.
       London: R. R. Laurie, 1872. (7th edition) vi,
       222p.

371. FINLASON, W. F.
      The History of the Jamaica Case [Negro rebellion,
      1865]. London: Chapman and Hall, 1869. xcvi,
      691p. (revised 2nd. edition?)

372. FISHER, Richard S.
      The Book of the World [descriptions of all coun-
      tries]. New York: Colton, 1849. 2 volumes.

373. FISKE, Amos Kidder (1842-1921)
      The West Indies [history and description]. New
      York: G. P. Putnam, 1899. xii, 414p.

374. FITZ GERALD, Edward Arthur (b. 1871)
      The Highest Andes. A Record of the First Ascent
      of Aconcagua and Tupungato in Argentina and the
      Exploration of the Surrounding Valleys [1896-8].
      New York: Charles Scribner's Sons, 1899. xvi,
      390p.; also London, 1899.

375. FITZROY, Robert (1805-65) (editor) (often listed
      under Charles Darwin)
      Narrative of the Surveying Voyage of His Majesty's
      Ships Adventure and Beagle [southern shores of
      South America, 1826-36]. Titles and editors vary.
      London: H. Colburn, 1839. 3 volumes. xxviii,
      597, xiv, 694, xiv, 615p. (Reprinted: New York,
      A. M. S. Press, 1971.)

376. FLANDERS, Mrs. (name variations: Flannigan,
      Lanaghan)
      Antigua and the Antiguans. London: The Author?
      1844. 2 volumes. xiv, 345, viii, 355p.

377. FLINT, Grover (1867-1909)
      Marching with Gómez; a War Correspondent's
      Field Notebook kept During four Months with the
      Cuban Army [1896]. Boston: Lamson Wolffe
      and Co., 1898. xxx, 290p.

378. FLINTER, Col. George Dawson (d. 1838)
      An Account of the Present State of the Island of
      Porto Rico. London: Longman?, 1819. xii,
      392p. (Reprinted: Westport, Negro Universities
      Press, 1971.)

379. FLINTER, Col. George Dawson
      History of the Revolution in Caracas.   London:
      T. and J. Allman, 1819.   xii, 212p.

380. FLIPPIN, John R.
      Sketches from the Mountains of Mexico.   Cin-
      cinnati: Standard Publishing Co., 1889.   xiv, 433p.

381. (FOLSOM, George) (1802-69)
      Mexico in 1842.   A Description of the Country....
      New York: C. J. Folsom, 1842.   256p.

382. FOOTE, Mrs. Henry Grant
      Recollections of Central America and the West
      Coast of Africa.   London: T. C. Newby, 1869.
      221p.

383. FOOTE, Henry Stuart (1804-80)
      Texas and the Texans [Mexican background; his-
      tory and description].   Philadelphia: Thomas
      Cowperthwait, 1841.   2 volumes.

384. FORBES, Alexander (pseud: "A Barrister")
      A History of Upper and Lower California [and
      description].   London: Smith, Elder and Co.,
      1839.   xvi, 352p.

385. FORBES, Alexander (pseud: "A Barrister")
      A Trip to Mexico, or Recollections of Ten Months
      Ramble in 1849-50.   London: Smith, Elder and
      Co., 1851.   256p.

386. FORD, Isaac Nelson (1848-1912)
      Tropical America [Mexico to Argentina].   New
      York: Charles Scribner's Sons, 1893.   xiv, 409p.

387. FOULKS, Theodore
      Eighteen Months in Jamaica, with Recollections
      of the Late Rebellion [1831-32].   London: Whit-
      taker, Treacher and Arnott, 1833.   123p.

388. FOUNTAIN, Paul
      The Great Mountains and Forests of South Amer-
      ica [1884-].   London: Longmans, Green, 1902.
      306p.

389.   (FRACKER, George)
       Voyage to South America, with an Account of a
       Shipwreck on the River La Plata in the Year 1817
       by the Sole Surviver. Boston: Ingraham and
       Hewes, 1826. vii, 128p.

390.   FRANCES, May
       Beyond the Argentine; or Letters from Brazil.
       London: W. H. Allen, 1890. viii, 148p.

391.   FRANKLIN, James
       The Present State of Hayti... [description]. Lon-
       don: John Murray, 1828. viii, 411p. (Reprint:
       New York, Negro Universities Press, 1970;
       London, Cass, 1971.)

392.   FRENCH, General Samuel Gibbs (1818-1910)
       Two Wars: An Autobiography of General...
       [Mexican War and Civil War experiences]. Nash-
       ville: Confederate Veteran Press, 1901. xv,
       404p.

393.   FROEBEL, Karl Ferdinand Julius (1805-93)
       Seven Years Travel in Central America, Northern
       Mexico... [etc.]. London: R. Bentley, 1859.
       587p. (first edition, 1853?)

394.   FROST, John (1800-59)
       Pictorial History of Mexico and the Mexican War
       [history and description]. Philadelphia: Thomas
       Cowperthwait, 1848. 652p.

395.   FROUDE, James Anthony (1818-94)
       The English in the West Indies, or the Bow of
       Ulysses [history, impressions]. New York:
       Charles Scribner's Sons, 1888. xii, 373p. (a
       London edition, 1888.) (Reprinted: Westport,
       Negro Universities Press, 1971.)

396.   FRUHBECK, Franz
       Brazilian Journey [1817-18]. Philadelphia: Uni-
       versity of Pennsylvania Press, 1960. 128p.

397.   FUENTES, Manuel Antanasio (b. 1820)
       Lima, or Sketches of the Capital of Peru [descrip-
       tive; hundreds of illustrations]. London: Trübner
       and Co., 1866. ix, 224p.

398. FURBER, George C.
      The Twelve Month Volunteer, or the Journal of a
      Private in the Tennessee Regiment of Cavalry
      [Mexican War; description, 1846-47].   Cincinnati:
      J. A. and N. P. James, 1848.   624p.

                        G

399. GALLENGA, Antonio Carlo Napoleone (1810-95)
      The Pearl of the Antilles [Cuba and Jamaica].
      London: Chapman and Hall, 1873.   202p. (Re-
      printed: Westport, Negro Universities Press,
      1971.)

400. GALLENGA, Antonio Carlo Napoleone
      South America [Oct. 21, 1879-June 1880; descrip-
      tion by London Times correspondent].   London:
      Chapman and Hall, 1880.   xii, 400p.

401. GALTON, Sir Francis (editor)
      Vacation Tourists and Notes of Travel [Latin
      America, etc. travel accounts, 1860-3].   London:
      Macmillan, 1861-4.   3 volumes.

402. GAMBLE, W. H.
      Trinidad, Historical and Descriptive [by a Baptist
      missionary].   London: Publisher unknown, 1866.
      120p.

403. GANVREAU, Charles F. (b. 1878)
      Reminiscences of the Spanish-American War in
      Cuba and the Philippines [description of Cuba].
      Rouses Point, New York: Authors' Publishing Co.,
      1915.   160p.

404. GARAY, José de (1801-58)
      An Account of the Isthmus of Tehuantepec in the
      Republic of Mexico [scientific surveys; people and
      places].   London: J. D. Smith and Co., 1846.
      viii, 128p.

405. GARCIA Cubas, Antonio (1830-1912)
      Mexico. Its Trade, Industries and Resources.
      Mexico: Dept. of Fomento, 1892.   xviii, 436p.
      (translated from Spanish.)

406.   GARCIA Cubas, Antonio
       Republic of Mexico in 1876.   Mexico: "La
       Enseñanzo, " 1876.   130p.   (translated from
       Spanish.)

407.   GARDINER, Capt. Allen Francis (1794-1851)
       A Visit to the Indians on the Frontiers of Chile
       [and Brazil and Argentina].   London: R. B.
       Seeley and W. Burnside, 1840.   194p.

408.   GARDINER, Capt. Allen Francis
       A Voice from South America.   London: Seeley,
       Burnside and Seeley, 1847.   iv, 107p.

409.   GARDNER, George (1812-49)
       Travels in the Interior of Brazil ... 1836-41
       [northern provinces; gold and diamonds].   London:
       Reeve Brothers, 1846.   xviii, 562.   (Reprinted:
       New York, A. M. S. Press, 1971.)

410.   GARDNER, William James
       A History of Jamaica [and description, 1492-1872].
       London: E. Stock, 1873.   xvi, 510p.   (Reprinted:
       London, Frank Cass, 1938.)

411.   GEIGER, John Lewis
       A Peep at Mexico.   Narrative of a Journey
       Across the Republic from the Pacific to the Gulf
       in December 1873 to January 1874.   London:
       Trübner and Co. , 1874.   xiv, 353p.

412.   "A GENTLEMAN"
       Notes on the Viceroyalty of La Plata... [descrip-
       tions, etc. , based on residence in Montevideo].
       London: J. J. Stockdale, 1808.   301p.

413.   GEORGE, Alfred
       Holidays at Home and Abroad [Mexico and United
       States].   London: W. J. Johnson, 1877.   xxiii,
       199p.

414.   GEORGE, Isaac (b. 1822)
       Heroes and Incidents of the Mexican War [and
       Mexican people and customs].   Greensburg: Re-
       view Publishing Co. , 1903.   296p.

415. GERSTACKER, Frederick Wilhelm Christian (1816-72)
      Gerstäcker's Travels: Rio de Janeiro, Buenos
      Aires, Ride through the Pampas, Winter Journey
      Across the Cordilleras, Chile, Valparaiso, Cali-
      fornia and the Gold Fields. London: Nelson and
      Sons, 1854. 624p.; and New York: Harper and
      Brothers, 1854. (translated from German.)

416. GERSTACKER, Frederick Wilhelm Christian
      How a Bride was won; or a Chase Across the
      Pampas. New York: D. Appleton and Co.,
      1869. 274p. (translated from German.)

417. GERSTACKER, Frederick Wilhelm Christian
      Narrative of a Journey Round the World... [Argen-
      tina, Chile, California, etc.]. London: Hurst and
      Blachett, 1853. 3 volumes. (translated from
      German.)

418. GIASFORD, Stephen
      An Essay on the Good Effects which May be
      Derived in the British West Indies in Consequence
      of the Abolition of the African Slave Trade. Lon-
      don: Publisher unknown, 1811. viii, 236p. (Re-
      printed: Westport, Negro Universities Press, 1971.)

419. GIBBS, Archibald Robertson
      British Honduras; an Historical and Descriptive
      Account of the Colony from its Settlement, 1670.
      London: Sampson Low, Marston, Searle and
      Rivington, 1883. viii, 198p.

420. GIBSON, Herbert
      The History and the Present State of the Sheep-
      breeding Industry in the Argentine Republic.
      Buenos Aires: Ravenscroft and Mills, 1893. x,
      297p.

421. (GIDDINGS, Luther)
      Sketches of the Campaign in Northern Mexico [by
      an officer in the Ohio Volunteer regiment; descrip-
      tions]. New York: G. P. Putnam, 1853. xii,
      336p.

422. GILLESPIE, Alexander
      Gleanings and Remarks Collected During Many

Months of Residence in Buenos Aires [1806-7].
London: B. Dewhurst, 1818. ii, 242p.

423. GILLIAM, Albert M. (d. 1859)
      Travels over the Table Lands and Cordilleras of
      Mexico During the Years 1843-44 [and California].
      Philadelphia: J. W. Moore, 1846. 455p.; also
      London: Wiley and Putnam, 1846. (London, 1847
      edition titled Travels in Mexico....)

424. GILLIES, Lt. James Melville (1811-65)
      The United States Naval Astronomical Expedition
      to the Southern Hemisphere during the Years 1849-
      52 [Chile, volume I]. Washington: A. D. P.
      Nicholson, 1852-58, 6 volumes. (Volume I on
      Chile published separately, Washington, 1855.
      xiii, 556p.)

425. GISBORNE, Lionel (1823-61)
      The Isthmus of Darien in 1852....   London:
      Saunders and Stanford, 1855. 238p.

426. GONZALEZ, Narciso Gener (1858-1903)
      In Darkest Cuba: Two Months Service under
      Gómez [1912?]. Columbia: State Publishing Co.,
      1922. 455p.

427. GOOCH, Fanny Chambers Ingelhart (1842-1913)
      Face to Face with the Mexicans [during seven
      years]. New York: Fords, Howard and Hulbert,
      1887. 584p. (Reprinted: brief edition, Carbon-
      dale, Southern Illinois University Press, 1867.
      xx, 248p.)

428. GOODALL, William
      Slavery and Anti-Slavery; a History of the Great
      Struggle in Both Hemispheres [North and South
      America; description]. New York: William
      Harned, 1852. x, 604p. (Reprinted: Westport,
      Greenwood, 1971.)

429. GOODHUE, Bertram Grosvenor (1869-1924)
      Mexican Memories. The Record of a Slight So-
      journ below the Yellow Rio Grande. New York:
      G. M. Allen, 1892. 167p.

430. GOODMAN, Walter (b. 1838)
      The Pearl of the Antilles, or, an Artist in Cuba.
      London: H. S. King and Co., 1873. xiv, 304p.

431. GOSSE, Philip Henry (1810-88)
      The Birds of Jamaica. London: J. Van Voorst,
      1847. x, 447p.

432. GOSSE, Philip Henry
      A Naturalist's Sojourn in Jamaica [18months].
      London: Longman, Brown, Green and Longmans,
      1851. xxiv, 508p.

433. GOTTSCHALK, Louis Moreau (1829-69)
      Notes of a Pianist; during ... Tours in the United
      States, Canada, the Antilles and South America....
      Philadelphia: J. B. Lippincott and Co., 1881.
      480p.

434. GRAHAM, Maria Dundas (Lady Maria Calcott) (1786-
      1842)
      Journal of a Residence in Chile During the Year
      1822 and a Voyage from Chile to Brazil in 1823.
      London: Longmans and Co., 1824. viii, 512p.
      (Reprinted: New York, Praeger, 1969.)

435. GRAHAM, Maria Dundas
      Journal of a Voyage to Brazil and a Residence
      there during part of the Years 1821, 1822, 1823.
      London: Longman, Hurst, Rees, Orme, Brown
      and Green, 1824. vi, 335p. (Reprinted: New
      York, Praeger, 1969.)

436. GRANT, Dr. Andrew
      History of Brazil: Narrative of Remarkable
      Events, Manners, Customs, Religion, etc. of the
      Natives; Cautions to Settlers, etc. London: H.
      Colburn, 1809. 304p.

437. GRAY, Albert Zabriskie (1840-89)
      Mexico as it is; being Notes on a Recent Tour
      in that Country. New York: E. P. Dutton and
      Co., 1878. 148p.

438. GREEN, Nathan C.
      Story of Spain and Cuba [description before War].

Baltimore: International News and Book Co.,
1896. 468p.

439.   GREEN, Thomas Jefferson (1801-63)
       Journal of the Texan Expedition against Mier.
       New York: Harper and Brothers, 1845.   487p.

440.   GREGG, Josiah (1806-50?)
       Commerce of the Prairies, or a Journal of a
       Santa Fe Trader [9 months residence in northern
       Mexico].   New York: H. G. Langley, 1844.   2
       volumes.   320, 318p.

441.   GREGG, Josiah
       Diary and Letters of... [1840-1850; Mexico,
       California].   Norman: University of Oklahoma
       Press, 1944-48.   2 volumes.   (edited by M. G.
       Fulton.)

442.   GRIFFIN, Solomon B. (b. 1852)
       Mexico Today.   New York: Harper and Brothers,
       1886.   viii, 267p.

443.   GRISWOLD, Chancey D.
       The Isthmus of Panama and What I Saw There.
       New York: Dewitt and Davenport, 1852.   180p.

444.   GRUBB, Wilfrid Barbrooke (1865-1930)
       An Unknown People in an Unknown Land [Uruguay,
       1889-].   Philadelphia: J. B. Lippincott, 1911.
       329p.   (also a London edition, 1911.)

445.   GUILLAUME, Herbert
       Amazon Provinces of Peru... [for European set-
       tlement, etc.].   London: Wyman and Sons, 1888.
       15, +309p.

446.   GURNEY, Joseph John (1788-1847)
       Familiar Letters to Henry Clay of Kentucky
       Describing a Winter in the West Indies.   London:
       John Murray, 1840.   xvi, 282p.   (also a New
       York edition, 1840.)   Title varies.   (Reprinted:
       Westport, Negro Universities Press, 1971.)

H

447. HACKETT, James
Narrative of an Expedition which Sailed from England in 1817 to Join the South American Patriots. London: John Murray, 1818. xv, 144p.

448. HADFIELD, William (1806-87)
Brazil, the River Plate and the Falkland Islands ... [1853]. London: Longman, Brown, Green and Longmans, 1854. vi, 384p.

449. HADFIELD, William
Brazil and the River Plate in 1868 [since 1853]. London: Bates, Hendy and Co., 1869. 271p.

450. HADFIELD, William
Brazil and the River Plate, 1870-76 [and Chile]. London: Edward Stanford, 1877. viii, 327p.

451. HAIGH, Samuel
Sketches of Buenos Aires and Chile. London: J. Carpenter and Son, 1829. xviiii, 316p.

452. HALE, Rev. Edward Everett (1822-1909) and Susan Hale (1833-1910)
A Family Flight Through Mexico. Boston: Lothrop and Co., 1886. 301p.

453. HALE, Susan (1833-1910)
The Story of Mexico [history and description]. New York: G. P. Putnam's Sons, 1888 (or 1889). xvi, 428p.

454. HALL, Arthur Daniel
Cuba. Its Past, Present and Future. New York: Street and Smith Publishers, 1898. 178p.

455. HALL, Arthur Daniel
Porto Rico. Its History, Products and Possibilities. New York: Street and Smith Publishers, 1898. 171p.

456. HALL, Capt. Basil (1788-1844)
Extracts from a Journal Written on the Coasts of Chile, Peru, and Mexico in the Years 1820, 1821,

1822. Edinburgh: Archibold Constable, 1824.
2 volumes. xx, 379, xii, 320, +80p. (also
Philadelphia and London editions, 1824.)

457. HALL, Col. Francis (d. 1833)
       Colombia. Its Present State.... London: Bald-
       win, Cradock and Joy, 1824. vi, 179p.

458. HALL, Thomas Winthrop (1862-1900)
       The Fun and Fighting of the Rough Riders [in
       Cuba during War with Spain]. New York: Fred-
       erick A. Stokes, 1899. viii, 242p.

459. HALL, William Henry Bullock (b. 1837)
       Across Mexico in 1864-5. London: Macmillan,
       1866. 396p.

460. HALLAM, George
       Narrative of a Voyage from Montego Bay, in the
       Island of Jamaica to England [1809].... Also a
       Voyage from England to Barbados... [1810].
       London: C. J. G. and F. Rivington, 1831. iv,
       112p.

461. HALLIDAY, Sir Andrew (1781-1839)
       The West Indies. The Natural and Physical
       History of the Windward and Leeward Colonies....
       London: J. W. Parker, 1837. viii, 408p.

462. HALPIN, Will R.
       Two Men in the West [Mexico]. Pittsburgh:
       Shaw Brothers, 1898. 108p.

463. HALSTEAD, Murat (1829-1908)
       The Story of Cuba. Her Struggles for Liberty...
       [history and description]. Chicago: The Werner
       Co., 1896. 503p.

464. HAMILTON, Col. John Potter (1777?-1873)
       Travels Through the Interior Provinces of Colom-
       bia. London: John Murray, 1827. 2 volumes.
       332, 256p.

465. HAMILTON, Leonidas Le Cenci
       Border States of Mexico [Sonora, Sinaloa, Chi-
       huahua, Durango]. San Francisco: Bacon and Co.,
       1881. 162p. (revised edition.)

466. HAMILTON, Leonidas Le Cenci
      Hamilton's Mexican Handbook [description]. Bos-
      ton: D. Lothrop and Co., 1883. 281p.

467. HAMILTON, Leonidas Le Cenci
      Hamilton's Mexican Law.... San Francisco:
      Bacon and Co. ? 1882. xiii, 327p.

468. HAMM, Margherita Arlina (1871-1907)
      Porto Rico and the West Indies. London: F.
      Tennyson Neely, 1899. 230p.

469. HANCOCK, Harrie Irving
      What One Man Saw [memoirs of a war corres-
      pondent in Cuba during War with Spain]. New
      York: Street and Smith, 1900. 177p.

470. (HANKSHAW, John)
      Letters Written from Colombia, During a Journey
      from Caracas to Bogotá and thence to Santa
      Martha in 1823. London: G. Cowie, 1823. xvi,
      208p.

471. HARDY, Lt. Robert William Hale (d. 1871)
      Travels in the Interior of Mexico in 1825, 1826,
      1827 and 1828 [Sonora, Baja California]. London:
      H. Colburn and R. Bentley, 1829. 540p.

472. HARRIS, J. Dennis
      A Summer on the Borders of the Caribbean Sea
      [Haiti]. New York: A. B. Burdick, 1860. 179p.
      (Reprinted: Ann Arbor, University of Michigan
      Press, 1970; Westport, Negro Universities Press,
      1971.)

473. HART, Daniel
      Trinidad and the West India Islands and Colonies.
      Trinidad: Chronicle Publishing Co., 1866. 250p.
      (second edition.)

474. HARTT, Charles Frederick (1840-78)
      Thayer Expedition. Scientific Results of a Journey
      in Brazil by Louis Agassiz and his Travelling
      Companions. Geology and Physical Geography of
      Brazil. Boston: Fields, Osgood and Co., 1870.
      xxiii, 620p.

475. HARTWIG, Dr. George Ludwig (1813-80)
      The Tropical World [flora and fauna in Mexico,
      South America, etc.]. London: Longman, Green,
      Longman, Roberts and Green, 1863. xx, 566p.

476. HARVEY, Thomas and William Brewin
      Jamaica in 1866. A Narrative of a Tour Through
      the Island.... London: C. Bennett, 1867. viii,
      126p.

477. HARVEY, William Woodis (1798-1864)
      Sketches of Hayti; from the Expulsion of the
      French to the Death of Christophe. London:
      L.B. Seeley and Son, 1827. xvi, 416p. (Re-
      printed: Westport, Negro Universities Press,
      1971.)

478. HASSAL, Mary (Mrs. Leonora Sansay)
      Secret History, or the Horrors of St. Domingo...
      [letters to Col. Burr]. Philadelphia: Bradford
      and Inskeep, 1808. 225p. (Reprinted: Westport,
      Negro Universities Press, 1971.)

479. HASSAUREK, Frederich (1832-85)
      Four Years Among Spanish-Americans [Ecuador,
      etc.]. New York: Hurd and Houghton, 1867. x,
      401p. (Reprinted: Carbondale, Southern Illinois
      University Press, 1967, abridged.)

480. HAVEN, Gilbert (1821-80)
      Our Next-Door Neighbor. A Winter in Mexico.
      New York: Harper and Brothers, 1875. 467p.;
      and New York: Nelson and Phillips, 1875.

481. HAWKSHAW, Sir John (1811-91)
      Reminiscences of South America: from Two and
      a Half Years Residence in Venezuela. London:
      Jackson and Walford, 1838. xii, 267p.

482. HAWTHORNE, Julian (1846-1934)
      Spanish America. New York: P.F. Collier,
      1889. 491p.

483. HAZARD, Samuel (1834-76)
      Cuba with Pen and Pencil. Chicago: Pitkin and
      Parker, 1871. 584p.; also editions in London
      and Hartford, 1871.

484. HAZARD, Samuel
      Santo Domingo, Past and Present, with a Glance
      at Hayti. New York: Harper and Brothers, 1873.
      xxx, 511p.; also edition in London, 1873.

485. HEAD, Sir Francis Bond (1793-1875)
      Reports Relating to the Failure of the Rio Plata
      Mining Association.... London: John Murray,
      1827. vii, 228p.

486. HEAD, Sir Francis Bond
      Rough Notes Taken During some Rapid Journeys
      Across the Pampas and Among the Andes [1825-6].
      London: John Murray, 1826. xii, 309p. (Re-
      printed: Carbondale, Southern Illinois University
      Press, 1967.)

487. HEARN, Lafcadio (1850-1904)
      Two Years in the French West Indies [especially
      Martinique, 1887-89]. New York: Harper and
      Brothers, 1890. 431p.

488. HEARN, Lafcadio
      Ycuma. The Story of a West Indian Slave. New
      York: Harper and Brothers, 1890. 193p. (Re-
      printed: New York, A.M.S. Press, 1969; St.
      Clair Shores, Scholarly Press, 1970.)

489. HEILPRIN, Angelo (1853-1907)
      The Bermuda Islands.... Philadelphia: The
      Author, 1889. viii, 231p.

490. HELMS, Anton Zacharias (Anthony Zachariah) (1751-
      1803)
      Travels from Buenos Aires by Potosí to Lima...
      [topographical and other descriptions]. London:
      R. Phillips, 1806. xii, 287p. (translated from
      German.)

491. HEMMENT, John C.
      Cannon and Camera. Sea and Land Battles of the
      Spanish-American War in Cuba. New York: Ap-
      pleton, 1898. xxi, 282p.

492. HENDERSON, James (1783?-1848)
      History of Brazil [1819 description]. London:
      Longman, Hurst, Rees, Orme and Brown, 1821.
      xxiii, 522p.

493.   HENRY, William Seaton (1816-51)
       Campaign Sketches of the War with Mexico.   New
       York: Harper and Brothers, 1847.   331p.

494.   HERNDON, Lt. William Lewis (1813-57) and Lt.
       Lardner Gibbon
       Exploration of the Valley of the Amazon [by two
       United States Naval Lieutenants].   Washington:
       R. Armstrong and A. O. P. Nicholson, 1853-54.
       2 volumes. iv, 414, x, 339p. (Volume 1 by
       Herndon, Volume II by Gibbon.) (Reprinted: New
       York, McGraw-Hill, 1952, abridged.)

495.   HERVEY, Maurice H.
       Dark Days in Chile.   An Account of the Revolution
       of 1891.   London: Edward Arnold, 1891?.   xii,
       331p.

496.   (HIBBERT, Edward)
       Narrative of a Journey from Santiago de Chile to
       Buenos Aires in July and August 1821.   London:
       John Murray, 1824.   146p.

497.   (HILL, Arthur S.) (pseud: "A Gringo")
       Through the Land of the Aztecs or Life and Travel
       in Mexico [under Díaz].   London: Sampson Low,
       Marston and Co., 1892.   x, 236p.

498.   HILL, Robert Thomas (b. 1858)
       Cuba and Porto Rico, with the Other Islands of
       the West Indies.   New York: Century Co., 1898.
       xxviii, 429p.

499.   HILL, S. S.
       Travels in Peru and Mexico [1849-50].   London:
       Longman, Green, Longmans and Roberts, 1860.
       2 volumes. xiv, 330, xii, 312p.

500.   HINCHLIFF, Thomas Woodbine (1825-82)
       Over the Sea and Far Away.   A Narrative of
       Wanderings Round the World [Brazil, Chile, etc.].
       London: Longmans, Green, 1876.   7, 327p.

501.   HINCHLIFF, Thomas Woodbine
       South American Sketches, or a Visit to Rio de
       Janeiro, the Organ Mountains, La Plata [etc.].

London: Longman, Green, Longman, Roberts, Green, 1863. xx, 414p.

502. HIPPISLEY, Gustavus
A Narrative of the Exposition to the Rivers Orinoco and Apuré [from England to join Patriot forces, 1817]. London: John Murray, 1818 (or 1819). xix, 653p.

503. HOBART-Hampden, Admiral Augustus Charles (also known as Hobart Pasha) (1822-86)
Sketches from My Life [seven chapters dealing with Argentina, Paraguay, Brazil, etc.]. Leipzig: B. Tauchnitz, 1887. 287p.

504. HOBBS, Capt. James (b. 1819)
Wild Life in the Far West... [Mexican wars with the United States and the French]. Hartford: Wiley, Waterman and Eaton, 1872. 488p. (Reprinted: Glorieta, Rio Grand Press, 1919.)

505. HODGSON, Capt. Studholme John (1805-90)
Truths from the West Indies [and Madeira, 1833]. London: W. Bell, 1838. xv, 372p.

506. HOLDEN, J.W.
A Wizard's Wanderings from China to Peru. London: Dean and Son, 1886. xvi, 170p.

507. HOLMES, William Henry (1846-1933)
Archaeological Studies Among the Ancient Cities of Mexico [Central Mexico and Yucatan; description]. Chicago: Field Columbian Museum, 1895. 338p. (Reprinted: New York, Kraus, 1968.)

508. HOLTON, Isaac Farwell
New Granada. Twenty Months in the Andes [Colombia, Venezuela, 1852-3]. New York: Harper and Brothers, 1857. 605p. (Reprinted: Carbondale, Southern Illinois University Press, 1967, abridged.)

509. HORNER, Gustavus R.B.
Medical Topography of Brazil and Uruguay. Philadelphia: Lindsey and Blakiston, 1845. 296p.

510. HOUSTOUN, Mrs. Matilda Charlotte (Jesse) Fraser
       (1815?-92)
            Texas and the Gulf of Mexico; or Yachting in the
            New World [before Mexican War]. London: J.
            Murray, 1844. 2 volumes.

511. HOVEY, Sylvester
            Letters from the West Indies [British and Danish
            islands]. New York: Gould and Newman, 1838.
            iv, 212p.

512. HOWARD, John Henry
            The Laws of the British Colonies in the West
            Indies... [slaves and slavery]. London: Colonial
            Office, 1827. 2 volumes in 1. xvi, 599, 386p.
            (Reprinted: Westport, Negro Universities Press,
            1971.)

513. HOWE, Julia Ward (1819-1910)
            A Trip to Cuba. Boston: Tickner and Fields,
            1860. iv, 251p. (Reprinted: New York, Praeger,
            1969; Westport, Negro Universities Press, 1971.)

514. HOWELL, Richard J.
            Mexico. Its Progress and its Commercial Pos-
            sibilities. London: W. B. Whittingham and Co.,
            1892. 203p.

515. HUDSON, William Henry (1841-1922)
            Idle Days in Patagonia. London: Chapman and
            Hall, 1893. vi, 256p. Many editions and varied
            titles.

516. HUDSON, William Henry
            The Naturalist in La Plata. London: Chapman and
            Hall, 1892. vii, 388p.

517. HUDSON, William Henry
            The Purple Land that England Lost... [Uruguay].
            London: Sampson Low, Marston, Searle and
            Rivington, 1885. 2 volumes. iv, 286, iv, 265p.

518. HUMBOLDT, Friedrich Heinrich Alexander von (1769-
       1859)
            The Island of Cuba. New York: Derby and Jack-
            son, 1856. 397p. (translated from Spanish.)
            (Reprinted: Westport, Negro Universities Press,
            1971.)

519. HUMBOLDT, Friedrich Heinrich Alexander von
Political Essays on the Kingdom of New Spain.
London: Longmans, 1811. 4 volumes. (trans-
lated from German.) (Reprinted: New York,
Knopf, 1972; abridged.)

520. HUMBOLDT, Friedrich Heinrich Alexander von
Researches Concerning the Ancient Inhabitants of
America, with Descriptions and Views of Striking
Scenes in the Cordelleras. London: Longman,
1814. 2 volumes. iv, 411, 432p. (translated
from French.)

521. HUMBOLDT, Friedrich Heinrich Alexander von and
Aimée Bonpland
Personal Narrative of Travels to the Equinoctial
Regions of the New Continent, During the Years
1799-1804. London: Longman, Hurst, Rees,
Orme and Brown, 1814-29. 7 volumes in 9.
(translated from French.) (Reprinted: New York,
Blom, 3 volumes, 1971.)

522. HUMPHREY, Alice R.
A Summer Journey in Brazil. New York: Bon-
nell and Silver, 1900. ix, 149p.

523. HUNTER, Daniel J. (pseud: Benjamín Vicuña Mac-
kenna) (1831-86)
A Sketch of Chile Expressly Prepared for the Use
of Immigrants from the United States and Europe.
New York: Haslett, 1866. 2 volumes in 1.

524. HUNTINGDON, Rev. Gurdon
The Shadowy Land, and other Poems, including
Guests of Brazil [description]. New York: D.
Dana, Jr., 1760. 506p.

525. HUNTINGTON, H.
A View of South America and Mexico by a Citizen
of the United States. New York: The Author?,
1825. (2 volumes in 1.)

526. (HURLBERT, William Henry) (1827-95)
Gen-Eden; or Pictures of Cuba. Boston: John P.
Jewett and Co., 1854. xii, 236p.; and New York:
Sheldon, Lamport and Blakeman, 1854.

527. HUTCHINSON, Thomas Joseph (1820-85)
      Buenos Aires and Argentine Gleanings, with Ex-
      tracts from the Diary of the Salado Exploration in
      1862 and 1863. London: Edward Stanford, 1865.
      xxi, 321p.

528. HUTCHINSON, Thomas Joseph
      Journey Through the Salado Valley [Argentina].
      London: Edward Stanford?, 1860.   ?p.

529. HUTCHINSON, Thomas Joseph
      The Paraná, with Incidents of the Paraguayan War
      and South American Recollections from 1861 to
      1868. London: Edward Stanford, 1868.   xxviii,
      424p.

530. HUTCHINSON, Thomas Joseph
      Two Years in Peru ... with Explorations of its
      Antiquities [1871]. London: Sampson Low, Mar-
      ston, Low and Searle, 1873.   2 volumes.   xxiv,
      343, xiii, 334p.

531. HYATT, Pulzski F.
      Cuba, Its Resources and Opportunities. Valuable
      Information for American Investors... [by United
      States Consul]. New York: J. S. Ogilvie Publish-
      ing Co., 1898.   222p.

                              I

532. IMRAY, James Frederick (1829?-1891)
      A Nautical Description of the Gulf of Mexico and
      Bay of Honduras [and Puerto Rico, Haiti, Cuba,
      Jamaica, Bahamas, etc.]. London: Imray and
      Son, 1856.   xii, 294p.   (7th edition) (several
      editions and titles.)

533. IM Thurn, Rev. Everard Ferdinand (1852-1932)
      Among the Indians of Guiana [British Guiana,
      1877-9, 1881-3?]. London: Kegan Paul, Trench
      and Co., 1883.   xviii, 445p.

534. IM Thurn, Rev. Everard Ferdinand
      Notes on the Indians of Guiana, 1878-79 [collection
      of 12 articles]. Georgetown: British Guiana
      Museum, 1878-79.   100p.

535. INARRAS, Domingo
Statistical and Commercial History of Guatemala.
London: Hearne, 1823. ?p. (translated from
Spanish.)

536. "AN INVALID" (pseud: H. H. N.)
A Winter in the West Indies and Florida... [de-
scription, observations, etc.]. New York: Wiley
and Putnam, 1839. ?p.

537. ISAACS, Jorge (1837-95)
María. A South American Romance [Colombia:
fiction; excellent description]. New York: Harper,
1890. 302p. (translated from Spanish.)

J

538. JACKSON, Julia Newell
A Winter Holiday in Summer Lands [Mexico].
Chicago: McClurgs, 1890. 221p.

539. JAMES, General Thomas (1782-1847)
Three Years Among the Indians and Mexicans
[1809 and 1821]. Waterloo, Ill: Office of War
Eagle, 1846. 316p. (Reprinted: Philadelphia,
J. B. Lippincott, 1962, abridged.)

540. JAMESON, Robert Francis (1766-1832)
Letters from the Havana During the Year 1820.
London: J. Miller, 1821. viii, 135p.

541. JAMIESON, Milton
Journal and Notes of a Campaign in Mexico [by
an Ohio volunteer; people and places]. Cincinnati: Ben Franklin Printing House, 1849. iv,
105p.

542. JAMISON, James Carson (1830-1916)
With Walker in Nicaragua [Reminiscences of an
officer]. Columbia, Mo.: E. W. Stephens, 1909.
181p.

543. JANVIER, Thomas Allibone (1849-1913)
The Mexican Guide. New York: Charles Scribner's Sons, 1885? xvi, 531p.

544. JANVIER, Thomas Allibone
      Stories of Old New Spain [Mexico].   New York:
      D. Appleton and Co., 1891. 326p.   (Reprinted:
      New York, Garrett Press, 1969.)

545. JARVES, James Jackson (1820-88)
      Scenes and Scenery in the Sandwich Islands, and
      a Trip Through Central America [in Central
      America, January and February, 1838].   Boston:
      J. Munroe and Co., 1843. 341p.

546. JAY, W. M. L. (pseud. for Julia Matilde Curtiss
      Woodruff, 1833-1909)
      My Winter in Cuba.   New York: E. P. Dutton and
      Co., 1871. 296p.

547. (JEBB, Mrs. John Beveridge Gladwyn)
      A Strange Career. Life and Adventures of John
      Gladwyn Jebb [in Brazil, Mexico, etc., by his
      widow].   Edinburgh: Blackwood, 1894? xxv,
      335p.

548. (JENKINS, John Edward) (1838-1910)
      The Coolie: His Rights and Wrongs [British
      Guiana].   London: Strahan and Co., 1871.   xii,
      446p.

549. JOHNSON, Daniel Noble (1822-63)
      The Journals of... [United States Navy; Brazil,
      Argentina, Uruguay, 1841-44].   Washington: The
      Smithsonian Institution, 1959.   vi, 268p.

550. JOHNSON, Edward Augustus (1860-1948)
      History of Negro Soldiers in the Spanish-Ameri-
      can War... [and description; Cuba].   Raleigh:
      Capital Printing Co., 1899. 147p.   (Reprinted:
      New York, Johnson Reprint Co., 1970.)

551. JOHNSON, Hannah More
      About Mexico, Past and Present.   Philadelphia:
      Presbyterian Board of Publications, 1887.   410p.

552. JOHNSON, Henry Charles Ross
      A Long Vacation in the Argentine Alps.   London:
      Richard Bentley, 1868.   viii, 180p.

553. JOHNSON, Theodore T. (b. 1818)
      California and Oregon; or Sights in the Gold Re-
      gions, and Scenes by the Way [Panama]. New
      York: Baker and Scribner, 1849. xii, 278p.

554. JOHNSTON, Samuel Burr
      Letters Written During a Residence of Three
      Years in Chile. Erie, Pa.: R. I. Curtis, 1816.
      205p.

555. JONES, John Matthew
      The Naturalist in Bermuda [geology, zoology,
      botany]. London: Reeves and Turner, 1859. xii,
      200p.

556. JONES, John Matthew and George Brown Goode
      (editors)
          Contributions to the Natural History of the
      Bermudas. Washington: Government Printing
      Office, 1884. xxiv, 353p.

557. JOSEPH, Edward Lanzer
      History of Trinidad [and description]. Trinidad:
      H. J. Mills, 1838. ix, 272p. (Reprinted: Lon-
      don, Frank Cass, 1970.)

558. JUARROS, Domingo (1752-1820)
      A Statistical and Commercial History of the King-
      dom of Guatemala... [general description]. Lon-
      don: J. Hearne, 1823. viii, 520. (translated
      from Spanish.) (Reprinted: New York, A. M. S.
      Press, 1971.)

                              K

559. KEENAN, Henry F.
      The Conflict with Spain. A History of the War
      Based on Official Reports and Eye-Witnesses
      [descriptions]. Philadelphia: P. W. Ziegler and
      Co., 1898. 594p.; also Chicago, 1898.

560. KEITH, Sir George Mouat
      A Voyage to South America and the Cape of Good
      Hope [in a British ship]. London: J. B. G. Vogel,
      1819. xxx, 119p. (first edition, London, 1810?)

561. KELLER-Leuzinger, Franz (1835-90)
      The Amazon and Madeira Rivers; Sketches and
      Descriptions from the Note-Book of an Explorer.
      London: Chapman and Hall, 1874. xvi, 177p.
      (also New York, D. Appleton, 1874.)

562. KENLY, John Reese (1822-91)
      Memoirs of a Maryland Volunteer. War with
      Mexico in the Years 1846, 1847, 1848 [Mexico].
      Philadelphia: J. B. Lippincott, 1873. 521p.

563. KENNAN, George (1845-1924)
      Campaigning in Cuba. New York: Century Co.,
      1899. vi, 269p. (Reprinted: Port Washington,
      Kennikat, 1971.)

564. KENNEDY, Andrew Jackson
      La Plata, Brazil and Paraguay During the Present
      War [by Royal Navy Officer]. London: Edward
      Stanford, 1869. vii, 273p.

565. KENNEDY, William (1799-1871)
      Texas: The Rise, Progress and Prospects of the
      Republic of Texas [before the War]. London: R.
      Hastings, 1841. 2 volumes.

566. KENNEDY, Sir William Robert (1838-1916)
      Sport, Travel and Adventure in Newfoundland and
      the West Indies [Haiti, Mosquito Coast]. London:
      W. Blackwood and Sons, 1885. x, 399p.

567. KENNEDY, Sir William Robert
      Sporting Adventures in the Pacific Whilst in Com-
      mand of the Reindeer [west coast of South America].
      London: Sampson Low, Marston, Searle and
      Rivington, 1876. 303p.

568. KENNEDY, Sir William Robert
      Sporting Sketches in South America [chiefly Argen-
      tina, Brazil]. London: R. H. Porter, 1892. xvi,
      268p.

569. KER, Henry
      Travels in the Western Interior of the United
      States... [and Mexico, 1808-16]. Elizabethtown,
      N. J.: The Author, 1816. 372p.

570. KERATRY, Count Emile de (1832-1904)
The Rise and Fall of the Emperor Maximilian [by
an observer]. London: Sampson Low, Son and
Marston, 1868. vii, 312p.

571. KERR, Sir John Graham (b. 1869)
A Naturalist in the Gran Chaco [1889-91, 1896-7].
Cambridge: Cambridge University Press, 1950.
xi, 234p. (Reprinted: New York, Greenwood,
1968.)

572. KIDDER, Rev. Daniel Parish (1815-91)
Sketches of a Residence and Travels in Brazil.
Philadelphia: Sorin and Ball, 1845. 2 volumes.
xv, 369, vii, 404p. (also London, Wiley and
Putnam, 1845, 2 volumes.)

573. KIDDER, Rev. Daniel Parish and Rev. James Cooley
Fletcher (1823-1901)
Brazil and the Brazilians Portrayed in Historical
and Descriptive Sketches. Philadelphia: Childs
and Peterson, 1857. 630p. (Reprinted: New
York, A. M. S. Press, 1969.)

574. KIMBALL, Richard Burleigh (1816-92)
Cuba and the Cubans. New York: G. P. Putnam,
1850. 255p.

575. KIMBALL, Richard Burleigh (pseud: "A Settler")
In the Tropics. By a Settler in Santo Domingo
[during 12 months]. New York: G. W. Carleton,
1863. 306p. (titled: Life in Santo Domingo,
1875.)

576. KING, David (1806-83)
The State and Prospects of Jamaica. London:
Johnstone and Hunter, 1850. xii, 235p.

577. KING, Col. John Anthony (b. 1803?)
Twenty-Four Years in the Argentine Republic
[under Rosas]. London: Longman, Brown, Green
and Longmans, 1846. xii, 442p.; New York:
Appleton, 1846. 324p. (abridged) (Reprinted:
New York, A. M. S. Press, 1971.)

578. KING, Philip Parker (1793-1856) and Robert Fitzroy
(1805-65)

Sailing Directions for South America [southern and western South America]. London: Hydrographic Office, Admiralty, 1850. xiv, 410p.

579. KINGSBOROUGH, Edward King (1795-1837)
Antiquities of Mexico [history, description, etc.]
London: R. Havell, 1830-48. 9 volumes.

580. KINGSLEY, Charles (1819-75)
At Last, A Christmas in the West Indies. London:
Macmillan, 1871. 2 volumes.

581. KINGSLEY, Tose Georgina
South by West; or, Winter in the Rocky Mountains
and Spring in Mexico. London: Isbister Co.,
1874. 411p.

582. KIRKE, Henry (1842-1925)
Twenty-Five Years in British Guiana [1872-97].
London: Sampson Low, Marston and Co., 1898.
xii, 364p. (Reprinted: Westport, Negro Universities Press, 1871.)

583. KNIGHT, Edward Frederick (b. 1852)
The Cruise of the "Falcon," A Voyage to South
America in a 30-ton Yacht [1880-2?]. London:
Sampson Low, Marston, Searle, Rivington and
Co., 1883. 2 volumes. viii, 301, vi, 304p.

584. KNOX, John P.
A Historical Account of St. Thomas, West Indies
[and description]. New York: Charles Scribner's
Sons, 1852. xii, 271p. (Reprinted: Westport,
Negro Universities Press, 1971.)

585. KNOX, Thomas Wallace (1835-96)
The Boy Travellers in Mexico. New York:
Harper and Brothers, 1890. xx, 552p.

586. KOLLONITZ, Paula (Condesa)
The Court of Mexico [Emperor Maximilian]. London: Saunders, Otlay and Co., 1867? 303p.
(translated from Austrian.)

587. KOSTER, Henry (d. 1820)
Travels in Brazil [1809-15]. London: Longman,

Hurst, Orme and Brown, 1817. 2 volumes. xii,
406, iv, 380p. (second edition?) (Reprinted:
Carbondale, Southern Illinois University Press,
1966, abridged.)

588. KROUPA, B.
      An Artist's Tour. Gleanings and Impressions of
      Travels in North and Central America and the
      Sandwich Islands. London: Ward and Downey,
      1890. xiv, 339p.

                          L

589. LAMBERT, Charles and Mrs. S.
      The Voyage of the "Wanderer" [Brazil, Uruguay,
      Chile, etc.; journals and letters]. London: Mac-
      millan, 1883. xx, 335p. (editor: Gerald Young.)

590. LANGSTON, John Mercer (1829-97)
      From the Virginia Plantation to the National
      Capital... [and descriptions of Haiti by the United
      States Minister in 1877]. Hartford: American
      Publishing Co. , 1894. 534p.

591. LANGWORTHY, Franklin (1798-1855?)
      Scenery of the Plains, Mountains and Mines
      [Western U. S. and Central America, 1850-53].
      Ogdensburg: J. C. Sprague, 1855. vi, 324p.

592. LARKIN, Frederick (b. 1814)
      Ancient Man in America... [United States and
      Central America history and description]. Ran-
      dolph, N. Y. : The Author, 1880. 276p.

593. LATHAM, Robert Gordon (1812-88)
      Man and His Migrations [including descriptions
      of Latin American Indians]. New York: C. B.
      Norton, 1852. 261p.

594. LATHAM, Wilfrid
      The States of the River Plate. Their Industries
      and Commerce.... London: Longmans, Green
      and Co. , 1866. vii, 200p.

595. LATROBE, Charles Joseph (1801-75)
      The Rambler in Mexico. New York: Harper and

Brothers, 1836.   viii, 309p.; and a London edition, 1836.

596. LAVAYSSE, M.
A Statistical, Commercial and Political Description of Venezuela, Trinidad, Margarite and Tobago. London: The Author? 1820. xxxix, 479p.

597. LAWRENCE-Arthur, James Henry (1823-89)
Monumental Inscriptions of the British West Indies... [people and families]. London: Chatto and Windus, 1875. xii, 442p.

598. LEE, Mrs. Hannah Farnham Sawyer (1780-1865)
Memoire of Pierre Toussaint, Born a Slave [Haitian descriptions]. Boston: Crosby, Nichols and Co., 1854. 124p. (second edition?) (Reprinted: Westport, Negro Universities Press, 1970.)

599. LEE, Mrs. S.M.
Glimpses of Mexico and California. Boston: Ellis, 1887. 124p.

600. LEMPRIERE, Charles (1818-1901)
Notes on Mexico in 1861 and 1862, Politically and Socially Considered. London: Longman, Green, Longmans, Roberts and Green, 1862. vi, 480p.

601. LE PLONGEON, Alice Dixon (b. 1851)
Here and There in Yucatan. New York: J.W. Bouton, 1886. iv, 146p.

602. LESTER, Charles Edwards (1815-90)
The Mexican Republic, an Historical Study [and description]. New York: The American News Co., 1875. 104p.

603. LEVER, Edward A.
Central America. New Orleans: E.A. Brandao, 1885. 293p.

604. LEWIS, Matthew Gregory (1775-1818)
Journal of a West India Proprietor [Jamaica, 1815-17]. London: John Murray, 1834. 408p. (Reprinted: Westport, Negro Universities Press, 1971.)

605. LEYLAND, J.
Adventures in the Far Interior of South Africa ...
and Rambles in Honduras. London: G. Routledge,
1866. vii, 282p.; also Liverpool, 1866.

606. LIGGETT, William, Sr.
My Seventy-Five Years Along the Mexican Border
[North Mexico, 1882-1960]. New York: Exposi-
tion Press, 1964. 139p.

607. LINDLEY, Thomas
Narrative of a Voyage to Brazil [Bahia, 1803].
London: J. Johnson, 1805. xxxi, 298p. (new
title, London: W. Baynes, 1808, revised.)

608. LIPPARD, George (1822-54)
Legends of Mexico [Mexican War]. Philadelphia:
T. B. Peterson, 1847. 136p.

609. LLOYD, Susette Harriet
Sketches of Bermuda. London: J. Cochrans,
1835. xv, 258p.

610. LLOYD, Dr. William
Letters from the West Indies, During a Visit in
the Autumn of 1836 and the Spring of 1837. London: Carton and Harvey, 1839. viii, 263p.

611. LOGAN, James
Notes of a Journey Through Canada, the United
States of America and the West Indies. Edinburgh:
Fraser and Co., 1838. vii, 259p.

612. LOMBARD, Thomas R.
The New Honduras, its Situation, Resources, etc.
New York: Brentano, 1887. 102p.

613. LOVE, George Thomas (pseud: "An Englishman")
A Five Year's Residence in Buenos Aires During
the Years 1820-1825. London: G. Herbert,
1825. viii, 176p.

614. LUCAS, Judge Daniel Bedinger (1836-1909)
Nicaragua: War of the Filibusters.... Richmond:
B. F. Johnson, 1896. 216p.

615. LUCCOCK, John
      Notes on Rio de Janeiro and the Southern Parts
      of Brazil [1808-18]. London: Samuel Leigh,
      1820. xv, 639p.

616. LUMHOLTZ, Karl Sofus (1851-1922)
      Unknown Mexico... [five years among the Indians;
      late 19th century]. New York: Charles Scribner's
      Sons, 1902. 2 volumes.

617. LUMMIS, Charles Fletcher (1859-1928)
      The Awakening of a Nation; Mexico Today. New
      York: Harper and Brothers, 1898. xiv, 179p.

618. LUMMIS, Charles Fletcher
      The Land of Poco Tiempo [Mexico; description].
      New York: Scribner, 1893. 310p.

619. LUNDY, Benjamin (1789-1839)
      The Life, Travels and Opinions of... [Mexico,
      Texas, Haiti, etc., before 1838]. Philadelphia:
      William D. Parrish, 1847. 318p. (edited by
      Thomas Earle.) (Reprinted: Westport, Negro
      Universities Press, 1971; and Clifton, N.J.,
      A.M. Kelley, 1971.)

620. LYDE, Lionel William (1863-1947)
      A Geography of North America, Including the West
      Indies. London: A. and C. Black, 1898. viii,
      116p.

621. LYDSTON, George Frank (1858-1923)
      Panama and the Sierras; A Doctor's Wander Days.
      Chicago: Riverton Press, 1900. 283p.

622. LYNCH, "Mrs. Henry" (Theodora Elizabeth) (1812-85)
      The Wonders of the West Indies. London: Seeley,
      Jackson and Halleday, 1856. 315p.

623. LYON, Capt. George Francis (1795-1832)
      Journal of a Residence and Tour in the Republic
      of Mexico in the Year 1826. London: John Mur-
      ray, 1828. 2 volumes. viii, 323, iv, 304p.
      (Reprinted: Port Washington, Kennikat, 1971.)

M

624. MACCANN, William
Two Thousand Miles Ride Through the Argentine
Provinces... [1848]. London: Smith, Elder, 1853.
2 volumes. xiv, 295, x, 323p. (Reprinted: New
York, A. M. S. Press, 1971.)

625. MACDOUALL, John
Narrative of a Voyage to Patagonia and Tierra del
Fuego, Through the Straits of Magellan in H. M. S.
Adventure and Beagle in 1826 and 1827. London:
Renshaw and Rush, 1833. iv, 320p.

626. MACERONI, Francis (1788-1846)
Memoirs of the Life and Adventures of... [Colom-
bia, etc.]. London: John Macrone, 1838. 2
volumes. 497, 509, xxip.

627. MACFARLANE, Thomas
To the Andes: Being a Sketch of a Trip to South
America.... Toronto: Balford Brothers, 1877.
174p.

628. MACGREGOR, Sir Gregor (1786-1845)
Some Account of the Mosquita Territory [Central
America]. Edinburgh: Publisher unknown, 1822.
?p.

629. MACGREGOR, John (also McGregor)
British America [Caribbean and Canada; description and history]. Edinburgh: William Blackwood,
1832. 2 volumes. xxii, 484, xiv, 605p.

630. MACGREGOR, John (also McGregor)
The States of Mexico; their Commerce, Trade....
London: C. Whiting, 1846. 305p.

631. MACKENZIE, Charles
Notes on Haiti, Made During a Residence in that
Republic [by the British Consul-General]. London:
H. Colburn and R. Bentley, 1830. 2 volumes.
xx, 335, 306p.

632. MACKIE, John Milton (1813-94)
From Cape Cod to Dixie and the Tropics [West

Indies]. New York: G. P. Putnam, 1864. 422p.
(Reprinted: Westport, Negro Universities Press,
1971.)

633. MACKINNON, Capt. Launchlan Bellingham (1815-77)
      Atlantic and Transatlantic Sketches, Afloat and
      Ashore [Canada, United States, West Indies].
      New York: Harper and Brothers, 1852. 324p.
      (abridged); also London: Colburn and Co. , 1852.
      2 volumes. xv, 288, ix, 292p.

634. MACKINNON, Capt. Launchlan Bellingham
      Steam Warfare on the Paraná [British and French
      ships]. London: Charles Ollier, 1848. xii, 302,
      vii, 287p.

635. MACLEOD, John (1777?-1820)
      Voyage of His Majesty's Ship Alcest... [Korea,
      China, Rio de Janeiro]. Philadelphia: M. Carey
      and Son, 1818. 224p.

636. MACQUEEN, James (1778-1870)
      The West India Colonies.... London: Baldwin,
      Cradock and Joy, 1824. xxvi, 427p. (Reprinted:
      Westport, Negro Universities Press, 1971.)

637. MACRAE, Archibald (1820-55)
      Report of Journeys Across the Andes and Pampas
      of the Argentine Provinces [1849-52; volume 2 of
      Gilliss report]. Washington: A. O. P. Nicholson,
      1855. ix, 300p.

638. MADDEN, Richard Robert (1798-1886)
      The Island of Cuba [description, etc.]. London:
      C. Gilpin, 1849. xxiv, 252p.

639. MADDEN, Richard Robert
      A Twelve month's Residence in the West Indies...
      [Jamaica, etc.]. Philadelphia: Carey, Lea and
      Blanchard, 1835. 2 volumes. xiv, 326, viii,
      434p. (Reprinted: Westport, Negro Universities
      Press, 1970.)

640. MAGOFFIN, Susan (Shelby) (1827-55)
      Down the Santa Fe Trail and into Mexico. The
      Diary of... [1846-47]. New Haven: Yale Univer-
      sity Press, 1926. xxv, 294p. (edited by Stella
      M. Drumm.)

641. MALER, Teobert (1842-1919)
Researches in the Central Portion of the Usumat-
sintla Valley [Maya history and description, 1898-
1900]. Cambridge: Peabody Museum, 1901.
volume 1. iv, 216p.

642. MANSFIELD, Charles Blackford (1819-55)
Paraguay, Brazil and the Plate [letters, 1852-3].
London: Macmillan and Co., 1856. xxii, 504p.
(Reprinted: A. M. S. Press, 1971.)

643. MARCOY, Paul (pseud. for Laurent Saint-Cricq)
A Journey Across South America from the Pacific
Ocean to the Atlantic Ocean. London: Blackie
and Sons, 1873. 2 volumes. xii, 524, viii, 496p.
(title varies) (translated from French.)

644. MARJORIBANKS, Alexander
Travels in South and North America [Brazil, etc.].
New York: D. Appleton, 1853. xiv, 480p.

645. MARKHAM, Sir Clements Robert (1830-1916)
Cuzco: A Journey to the Ancient Capital of
Peru... [1852]. London: Chapman and Hall,
1856. iv, 419p.

646. MARKHAM, Sir Clements Robert
Peru [history and description]. London: Sampson Low, Marston, Searle and Rivington, 1880.
viii, 192p.

647. MARKHAM, Sir Clements Robert
The War Between Peru and Chile, 1879-82 [history
and description]. London: Sampson Low, Marston,
Searle and Rivington, 1883. xii, 306p.

648. MARKHAM, Sir Clements Robert
Travels in Peru and India. London: John Murray, 1862. xviii, 572p.

649. MARRYAT, Frederick (1792-1848)
The Travels and Adventures of Monsieur Violet,
in California, Sonora and Western Texas. London:
Longman, Brown, Green and Longmans, 1843.
365p.

650. MARRYAT, Joseph (1757-1824)
      An Examination of the Report of the Berbice Com-
      missioners [description of British Crown estates
      in Guiana]. London: Hughes and Baynes, 1817.
      122p.

651. MARRYAT, Joseph
      More Thoughts Still on the State of the West India
      Colonies [Grenada, etc.]. London: J.M. Richard-
      son, 1818. 147p.

652. MARTIN, Robert Montgomery (1803?-68)
      History of the West Indies [and description]. Lon-
      don: Whitaker, 1836-7. 2 volumes. xxxvi, 308,
      viii, 344p.

653. MARTIN, T. E.
      Hermosa, or in the Valley of the Andes. A Tale
      of Adventure. London: S. Low, Marston, Searle
      and Rivington, 1887. 2 volumes.

654. MASON, R. H.
      Picture of Life in Mexico. London: Smith,
      Elder, 1851 (or 1852). 2 volumes.

655. MASTERMAN, George Frederick
      Seven Eventful Years in Paraguay [Paraguayan
      War]. London: Sampson Low, Son and Marston,
      1869. xvi, 356p.

656. MASTERS, George Chaworth (1841-79)
      At Home with the Patagonians. London: John
      Murray, 1871. xx, 322p.

657. MATHEWS, Edward Davis
      Up the Amazon and Madeira Rivers, Through
      Bolivia and Peru [railroad engineer in 1870s].
      London: S. Low, Marston, Searle and Rivington,
      1879. xvi, 402p.

658. MATHISON, Gilbert Farquhar
      Narrative of a Visit to Brazil, Chile, Peru and
      the Sandwich Islands [1821-2]. London: C.
      Knight, 1825. xii, 478p.

659. MATTHEWS, Albert Franklin (1858-1917)
      The New Born Cuba. New York: Harper and
      Brothers, 1899. xii, 388p.

660.   MAUDSLEY, Anne Cary Morris and Alfred Percival
       (b. 1850)
       A Glimpse at Guatemala and Some Notes on the
       Ancient Monuments of Central America.   London:
       John Murray, 1899.   xvii, 289p.

661.   MAWE, John (1764-1829)
       Travels in the Interior of Brazil, Particularly in
       the Gold and Diamond Districts of that country
       [and Uruguay, La Plata, 1805-10].   London: Long-
       man, Hurst, Rees, Orme and Brown, 1812.   vii,
       368p.

662.   MAWE, John
       Travels in the Gold and Diamond Districts of
       Brazil [and Peru and Chile].   London: Longman,
       Hurst, Rees, Orme and Green, 1825.   x, 483p.

663.   MAXIMILIAN I, Emperor of Mexico (Ferdinand Maxi-
       milian Joseph) (1832-67)
       Recollections of My Life [Brazil, 1859-60 in
       volume 3].   London: Richard Bentley, 1868.   3
       volumes.

664.   MAY, Lt. Henry Lister
       Journal of a Passage from the Pacific to the
       Atlantic [Marañón and Amazon to Pará, 1827].
       London: John Murray, 1829.   xv, 486p.

665.   MAYER, Brantz (1809-79)
       Mexico, as it was and is.   New York: J. Win-
       chester, 1844.   390p.; and London: Wiley and
       Putnam, 1844.

666.   MAYER, Brantz
       Mexico.   Aztec, Spanish and Republican [history
       and description].   Hartford: S. Drake and Co.,
       1851.   2 volumes.   433, 399p.

667.   MCCALLUM, Pierre F.
       Travels in Trinidad During the Months of Febru-
       ary, March and April, 1803.   Liverpool: W.
       Jones, 1805.   354p.

668.   MCCARTY, Rev. J. Hendrickson
       Two Thousand miles Through the Heart of Mexico.
       New York: Hunt and Eaton, 1886.   288p.

669. MCCOLLESTER, Sullivan Holman (1826-1921)
      Mexico Old and New. A Wonderland. Boston:
      Universalist Publishing House, 1897. vi, 266p.

670. MCCOOK, Henry C.
      The Martial Graves of our Fallen Heroes in
      Santiago de Cuba [description]. Philadelphia:
      Jacobs, 1899. 448p.

671. MCDONNELL, Alexander
      Considerations of Negro Slavery [Trinidad, Demera-
      ra, etc.]. London: Longman, Hurst, Rees, 1824.
      xiv, 338p.

672. MCINTOSH, Burr
      The Little I Saw of Cuba. New York: Neely,
      1899. 173p.

673. MCKINNON, Daniel (d. 1830)
      A Tour Through the West Indies in the Years
      1802 and 1803 [British]. London: S. Wolmer,
      1804. viii, 272p.

674. MCQUADE, James
      The Cruise of the Montauk to Bermuda, the West
      Indies and the Islands. New York: Thomas R.
      Knox and Co., 1885. xvi, 441p.

675. MCSHERRY, Richard (1817-85)
      El Puchero: or, a Mixed Dish from Mexico
      [Mexican war; country and people]. Philadelphia:
      J. B. Lippincott, Grambo, 1850. 247p.

676. MELISH, John
      A Geographical Description of the United States
      with the contiguous British and Spanish Posses-
      sions [Mexico]. Philadelphia: The Author, 1816.
      182p. (several subsequent editions.)

677. MERWIN, Mrs. C. B. (pseud: "A Lady of Ohio")
      Three Years in Chile [1853-   ]. Columbus, Ohio:
      Follett, Foster and Co., 1861. viii, 158p. (Re-
      printed: Carbondale, Southern Illinois University
      Press, 1967.)

678. MICHLER, Lt. N.
      Report of Survey for an Inter Ocean Ship Canal

Near the Isthmus of Darien. Washington: Government Printing Office, 1850. 2 volumes.

679. MIERS, John (1789-1879)
Travels in Chile and La Plata [1819-35]. London: Baldwin, Cradock and Joy, 1826. 2 volumes. xvi, 494, viii, 532p. (Reprinted: New York, A. M. S. Press, 1970.)

680. MILEY, John David
In Cuba with Schafter [experiences and descriptions]. New York: Scribners, 1899. xi, 228p.

681. MILL, Nicholas
History of Mexico from Spanish Conquest to Present Era [early 19th century description]. London: Sherwood, Jones Co., 1824. 300p.

682. MILLER, Archibald T.
Seaboard Sketches in the West Indies and South America. Liverpool: Publisher unknown, 1888. ?p.

683. MILLER, Joaquin (1839-1913)
Songs of the Mexican Seas. Boston: Roberts Brothers, 1887. 132p.

684. MILLER, Joaquin
Songs of the Sierras [Mexico, Nicaragua, California]. Boston: Roberts Brothers, 1871. 299p.

685. MILLER, John (editor)
The Memoirs of General [William] Miller in the Service of the Republic of Peru [under San Martín; William lived 1795-1861]. London: Longman, Rees, Orme, Brown and Green, 1828. 2 volumes. lii, 452, vii, 557p. (Reprinted: New York, A. M. S. Press, 1969.)

686. MILLICAN, Albert
Travels and Adventures of an Orchid Hunter in Colombia. London: Cassell, 1891. xv, 222p.

687. MITCHELL, Bess
Cortés, Montezuma and Mexico Past and Present... [and future; description]. Chicago: A. Flanagan, 1898. 139p.

688.   M'MAHON, Benjamin
       Jamaica Plantership [descriptions and indictment
       by an 18 years resident]. London: Publisher un-
       known, 1839. 304p.

689.   MOISTER, William (1808-91)
       Memorials of Missionary Laborours in Africa and
       the West Indies. New York: Lane and Scott,
       1851. 348p. (London edition, 1850?)

690.   MOISTER, William
       The West Indies, Enslaved or Free [history and
       description]. London: T. Woolmer, 1883. 394p.

691.   MOLLIEN, Gaspar Théodore (Compte de) (1796-1872)
       Travels in the Republic of Colombia [1822-23].
       London: C. Knight, 1824. iv, 460p. (translated
       from French.)

692.   MONTAGNAC, Nöel de
       Negro Nobodies: Being a Series of Sketches of
       Peasant Life in Jamaica. London: T. F. Unwin,
       1899. 212p.

693.   MONTGOMERY, George Washington (1804-41)
       Narrative of a Journey to Colombia... [1838].
       New York: Wiley and Putnam, 1839. 8, +175p.

694.   MONTGOMERY, James (1771-1854)
       The West Indies, and other Poems [in honor of
       abolition of slave trade, 1807]. Morris-town:
       Peter A. Johnson, 1811. 159p.

695.   MONTULE, Edouard de
       A Voyage to North America and the West Indies
       in 1817. London: Sir Phillips and Son, 1821.
       102p.

696.   MOORE, Henry (editor)
       Railway Guide to the Republic of Mexico [descrip-
       tions]. Springfield: Huben and Moore, 1894.
       318p. (in English and Spanish.)

697.   MORANT, George C.
       Chile and the River Plate in 1891. London:
       Waterlow and Sons, 1891. 268p.

698. MORELET, Arthur (b. 1809)
Travels in Central America. New York: Leypoldt,
Holt and Williams, 1871. 430p. (translated and
abridged from French edition, 2 volumes, by Mrs.
E. G. Squier.)

699. MORLAN, Albert
A Hoosier in Honduras. Indianapolis: El Dorado
Publishing Co. , 1897. 215p.

700. "MORLEY, Helena" (pseud. for Alice Dayrell Bryant)
The Diary of... [Brazil, 1893-95]. New York:
Straus and Cudahy, 1957. 281p. (translated from
Portuguese.)

701. MORRIS, Charles (1833-1927)
Our Island Empire [Cuba, Puerto Rico, Hawaii,
Philippines; description]. Philadelphia: J. B.
Lippincott, 1899. 488p.

702. MORRIS, Sir Daniel (b. 1844)
The Colony of British Honduras. London: Edward
Stanford, 1883. xiv, 152p.

703. MORRIS, Ira Nelson (1875-1942)
With the Trade-Winds. A Jaunt in Venezuela and
the West Indies. New York: G. P. Putnam's Sons,
1897. x, 157p.

704. MORTIMER, William Golden
Peru. History of Cocoa, "The Divine Plant of
the Incas" [description about 1895-1900]. New
York: J. H. Vail and Co. , 1901. xxxii, 576p.

705. MOUNTENEY, Thomas J. Barclay de (editor)
Selections from the Various Authors who have
Written Concerning Brazil [Minas Geraes, gold
mines, etc.]. London: Effingham Wilson, 1825.
xii, 182.

706. MULHALL, Mrs. Marion McMurrough
Between the Amazon and the Andes, or Ten Years
of a Lady's Travel [Argentina, Uruguay]. London:
Edward Stanford, 1881. xi, 340p.

707. MULHALL, Mrs. Marion McMurrough
From Europe to Paraguay and Matto-Grosso. London: Edward Stanford, 1877. 116p.

708.   MULHALL, Michael George (1836-1900)
       The Cotton Fields of Paraguay and Corientes [tour,
       1862-4]. Buenos Aires: M. G. and E. T. Mulhall,
       1864. 120p.

709.   MULHALL, Michael George
       The English in South America [history and descrip-
       tion]. London: Edward Stanford, 1878. 641p.;
       also Buenos Aires: "Standard," 1878.

710.   MULHALL, Michael George
       Handbook of Brazil. Buenos Aires: "Standard,"
       1877. 236p.

711.   MULHALL, Michael George and E. T.
       Handbook of the River Plate [Argentina, Uruguay,
       Paraguay]. Buenos Aires: "Standard," 1863.
       687?p. Many subsequent editions.

712.   MULHALL, Michael George
       Rio Grande do Sul [and its German colonies, 1871].
       London: Longmans, Green and Co., 1873. vi,
       202p.

713.   MURRAY, The Honorable Amelia Matilda (1795-1884)
       Letters from the United States, Cuba and Canada.
       London: J. W. Parker, 1856. 2 volumes. New
       York: Putnam, 1856. 1 volume. 402p. (Re-
       printed: Westport, Negro Universities Press, 1
       volume, 1969.)

714.   MURRAY, Sir Charles Augustus (1806-95)
       Travels in North America... [Cuba included].
       London: Robert Bentley, 1854. 2 volumes.

715.   MURRAY, Capt. Henry A.
       Lands of the Slave and the Free; or Cuba, United
       States and Canada. London: John W. Parker and
       Son, 1855. 2 volumes. 980p.

716.   MURRAY, Hugh
       An Encyclopedia of Geography [including North
       and South America]. London: Longmans, 1834.
       xii, 1567p.

717.   MURRAY, Rev. John Hale
       Travels in Uruguay [sheep farming, immigration,

1868-]. London: Longmans and Co. , 1871.
viii, 234p.

718. MUSGRAVE, George Clarke
      Under Three Flags in Cuba.   Boston: Little,
      Brown, 1899.   xv, 365p.

719. MUSICK, John R.
      Lights and Shadows of our War with Spain [anec-
      dotes, sketches, etc.].   New York: J. S. Ogilvie,
      1898.   224p.

720. MUSTERS, George Chaworth (1841-79)
      At Home with the Patagonians.   A Year's Wander-
      ings over Untrodden Ground from the Straits of
      Magellan to the Rio Negro [during one year].
      London: John Murray, 1871.   xx, 322p.   (Re-
      printed: New York, Greenwood, 1969.)

721. MYERS, Henry Morris and Philip Van Ness Myers
      (1846-1937)
      Life and Nature Under the Tropics, or Sketches of
      Travels among the Andes and on the Orinoco, Río
      Negro, Amazons [and Honduras, 1867-70].   New
      York: D. Appleton and Co. , 1871.   xvi, 330p.

722. MYERS, Capt. John
      The Life, Voyages and Travels of... [Pacific
      coasts of North and South America].   London:
      Longman, Hurst, Rees and Co. , 1817.   410p.

                          N

723. NADAILLAC, Marquis de (Jean François Albert de
      Ponget) (1818-1904)
      Pre-Historic America [Peru, Central America,
      description].   London: G. P. Putnam's, 1884.
      xii, 566p.   (translated from French.)   (Reprinted:
      New York, Humanities Press, 1970.)

724. NAPP, Richard
      The Argentine Republic.   Buenos Aires: Sociadad
      Anónima?   1876.   xcvii, 463p.   (translated from
      German.)

725. NEELY, F. Tennyson
      Neely's Spanish American War Panorama [photo-
      graphs and descriptions]. New York: The Author,
      1898. 170p.

726. NELSON, Wolfred (1846-1913)
      Five Years at Panama. The Trans-Isthmenian
      Canal. New York: Belford Co. , 1889. xiv,
      287p.

727. NEWBERY, Diego (pseud. for George Harkness)
      Pampa Grass; The Argentine Story as Told by an
      American Pioneer to his Son [George Harkness
      Newbery in Argentina in 1880s]. Buenos Aires:
      Editorial Guaraní, 1953. 558p.

728. NICHOLS, Benito
      Nichols' Guide to Mexico. Commercial and Offi-
      cial Guide to the Republic of Mexico. Mexico
      City: B. Nichols, 1884. 144p.

729. NIEDERLEIN, Gustavo (b. 1858)
      The Republic of Costa Rica [description, etc.].
      Philadelphia: Philadelphia Commercial Museum,
      1898. 127p.

730. NILES, John Milton (pseud: "Citizen of the United
      States") (1787-1856)
      A View of South America and Mexico [history and
      description]. New York: Huntington Jr. , 1825.
      2 volumes.

731. NISSEN, Johan Peter
      Reminiscences of a 46 Year's Residence in the
      Island of St. Thomas in the West Indies. Naza-
      reth, Pa.: Senseman and Co. , 1838. 228p.

732. NOBLE, Adeline M. (Ferriss)
      Rambles in Cuba. New York: Publisher unknown,
      1870. 136p.

733. NOLL, Arthur Howard (1855-1930)
      A Short History of Mexico [and description].
      Chicago: A. C. McClurg, 1890. 294p.

734. NORDHOFF, Charles (1830-1901)
      Peninsular California [northern half of Baja Cali-

fornia]. New York: Harper and Brothers, 1888.
130p.

735. NORIE, John William (1772-1843)
West India Directory [navigation; Florida to Gulf
of Pará through West Indies]. London: J. W.
Norie and Co., 1827-29. 4 parts in 1 volume.

736. NORMAN, Benjamin Moore (1809-60)
Rambles by Land and Water, or Notes of Travel
in Cuba and Mexico. New York: Paine and
Burgess, 1845. 216p.

737. NORMAN, Benjamin Moore
Rambles in Yucatan, or Notes of Travel through
the Peninsula. New York: Henry G. Langley,
1842. 304p.

738. "North, Oliver" (pseud. for W. Mullen)
Rambles after Sport; or Travels and Adventures
in the Americas and Home [Mexico, West Indies,
Chile, United States]. London: The "Field"
Office, 1874. 268p.

739. NORTON, Col. Lewis Adelbert (b. 1819)
Life and Adventures of... [during Mexican War,
etc.]. Oakland: Pacific Press Publishing House,
1887. 492p.

740. NUGENT, Lady Maria (Skinner) (d. 1834)
A Journal of a Voyage to, and a Residence in,
Jamaica from 1801 to 1805. London: T. W.
Boone, 1839. 2 volumes.

741. NUÑEZ, Ignacio Benito (1792-1846) (editor)
An Account, Historical, Political and Statistical,
of the United Provinces of Rio de la Plata... [a
symposium]. London: R. Akermann, 1825. x,
345p. (translated from Spanish.)

742. NUTTALL, Thomas (1786-1859)
The Genera of North American Plants [including
South America, West Indies]. Philadelphia: D.
Heartt, 1818. 2 volumes. viii, 312p, 254, +14p.
(Reprinted: New York, Hafner, 1971.)

O

743.   OBER, Frederick Albion (1849-1913)
       Camps in the Caribbees. The Adventures of a
       Naturalist in the Lesser Antilles. Boston: Lee
       and Shepard, 1880. xviii, 366p.

744.   OBER, Frederick Albion
       The Knockabout Club in the Antilles and there-
       abouts [juvenile; description]. Boston: Estes
       and Lauriat, 1888. 239p.

745.   OBER, Frederick Albion
       The Knockabout Club on the Spanish Main [juvenile;
       description]. Boston: Estes and Lauriat, 1891.
       239p.

746.   OBER, Frederick Albion
       Porto Rico and its Resources. New York: D.
       Appleton, 1899. 282p.

747.   OBER, Frederick Albion
       Travels in Mexico and Life Among the Mexicans
       [9 months]. Boston: Estes and Lauriat, 1884.
       672p.

748.   OBER, Frederick Albion
       Under the Cuban Flag, or the Cacique's Treasure
       [juvenile; description]. Boston: Estes and Lauriat,
       1897. 316p.

749.   O'KELLY, James J.
       The Mambi-Land, or Adventures of a Herald Cor-
       respondent in Cuba. Philadelphia: J.B. Lippin-
       cott, 1874. 359p.; also London, 1874.

750.   O'LEARY, Daniel Florencio (1800-54)
       Bolívar and the Wars of Independence. Memorias
       del General Florencio O'Leary [1783-1826].
       Austin: University of Texas Press, 1970. xx,
       386p. (abridged, edited, translated by Robert F.
       McNerney, Jr. from 32 volumes, Caracas, 1879-
       88.)

751.   OLIPHANT, Laurence (1829-88)
       Patriots and Filibusters [Central America, etc.].
       London: W. Blackwood and Sons, 1860. viii, 242p.

752. OLIVARES, José de
      Our Islands and their People as seen with Camera
      and Pencil [Cuba, Puerto Rico, etc.].   New York:
      N. D. Thompson Publishing Co., 1899.   2 volumes.
      (widely printed.)

753. OLIVER, Vere L.
      The History of the Island of Antigua [and geneolo-
      gies and society].   London: Publisher unknown,
      1849-99.   3 volumes.

754. ORTON, James (1830-77)
      The Andes and the Amazon, or Across the Con-
      tinent of South America [Ecuador to Pará on
      Smithsonian Expedition, 1867-].   New York:
      Harper and Brothers, 1870.   356p.

755. OSWALD, Felix Leopold (1845?-1906)
      Adventures in Cuba, or How an American Boy
      Saved his Friend and Escaped from a Spanish
      Prison [juvenile; description].   New York: W. L.
      Allison, 1898.   206p.

756. OSWALD, Felix Leopold
      Days and Nights in the Tropics.   Boston: D.
      Lothrop, 1887.   186p.

757. OSWALD, Felix Leopold
      Summerland Sketches, or Rambles in the Back-
      woods of Mexico and Central America.   Phila-
      delphia: J. B. Lippincott, 1880.   425p.

758. OSWANDEL, J. Jacob
      Notes on the Mexican War, 1846-47-48 [Journal of
      volunteer; campaigns, people, places].   Philadel-
      phia: The Author, 1885.   642p.

759. OTIS, Fessenden Nott (1825-1900)
      Illustrated History of the Panama Railroad [a
      guide].   New York: Harper and Brothers, 1862.
      263p.   (titled: Isthmus of Panama, 1867.)   (Re-
      printed: New York, A. M. S. Press, 1971.)

760. OTIS, Fessenden Nott
      Isthmus of Panama.   History of the Panama Rail-
      road [guide for travelers and businessmen].   New
      York: Harper, 1867.   317p.

761. OUSELEY, William Gore (1797-1866)
      Description and Views of South America [Bahia,
      Rio de Janeiro, Montevideo, Buenos Aires]. Lon-
      don: Thomas McLean, 1852. viii, 118p.

                              P

762. PAEZ, Ramón
      Wild Scenes in South America. Life in the Llanos
      of Venezuela. New York: Charles Scribners,
      1862. x, 502p.; new title: Travels and Adven-
      tures..., New York: Scribners, 1868.

763. PAGE, Thomas Jefferson (1808-99)
      La Plata, the Argentine Confederation and Para-
      guay [1853-6, by officer United States Navy].
      New York: Harper and Brothers, 1859. xvi, 632p.;
      also London edition, 1859.

764. PALGRAVE, William Gifford (1826-88)
      Dutch Guiana. New York: Macmillan Co., 1876.
      viii, 364p. (Reprinted: Westport, Negro Univer-
      sities Press, 1971.)

765. PARISH, Sir Woodbine (1791-1882)
      Buenos Aires and the Provinces of the Río de la
      Plata [1824-32]. London: John Murray, 1839.
      xxviii, 415p.

766. PATON, William Agnew (1848-1918)
      Down the Islands. A Voyage to the Caribbean.
      New York: Charles Scribner's Sons, 1887. xiv,
      301p. (Reprinted: Westport, Negro Universities
      Press, 1971.)

767. PAYNE, A. R. Middleton
      The Geral-Milco; or, the Narrative of a Residence
      in a Brazilian Valley of the Sierra Paricis [dis-
      covery of a tribe of Indians; fantasy?]. New York:
      Charles B. Norton, 1852. 264p.

768. PAYNE, A. R. Middleton
      Rambles in Brazil, or, a Peep at the Aztecs by
      One Who has Seen them [fantasy? and description].
      New York: C. B. Norton, 1854. 264p.

769. PAYNE, Will and Charles T. W. Wilson
      Missionary Pioneering in Bolivia, with Some Ac-
      count of Work in Argentina [late nineteenth cen-
      tury]. London: H. A. Raymond, 1904? 148p.

770. PAZOS Kanki, Vicente (1780?-1851?)
      Letters on the United Provinces of South America
      [to Henry Clay]. New York: J. Semour, 1819.
      259p.; also London: H. Miller, 1819. (trans-
      lated from Spanish.)

771. PEABODY, George Augustus (1831-1929)
      South American Journals of... [Argentina, Chile,
      1855-59]. Salem: Peabody Academy of Science,
      1937. xvi, 209p.

772. PECK, George Washington (1817-59)
      Melbourne, and the Chincha Islands: with
      Sketches of Lima.... New York: Charles Scrib-
      ner, 1854. 294p.

773. PECK, John James (1819-78)
      The Sign of the Eagle. A View of Mexico, 1830
      to 1855 [his letters, August 26, 1845 to April 14,
      1848]. San Diego: Union-Tribune Publishing Co.,
      1970. xiv, 168p.

774. PELLESCHI, Giovanni (or Juan)
      Eight Months on the Gran Chaco of the Argentine
      Republic [1879?]. London: Sampson Low, Mars-
      ton, Searle and Rivington, 1886. xvi, 311p.

775. PEÑAFIEL, Antonio (1831-1921)
      Monuments of Ancient Mexican Art. Ornaments,
      Mythology, Tributes... [description]. Berlin:
      A. Ashur and Co., 1890. 3 volumes. (in Eng-
      lish, French and Spanish.)

776. PEPPER, Charles Melville (1859-1930)
      Tomorrow in Cuba. New York: Harper and
      Brothers, 1899. vii, 316p.

777. PEREZ Triana, Santiago (1858-1916)
      Down the Orinoco in a Canoe. New York: T. Y.
      Crowell, 1902. xv, 253p.; first edition in
      Spanish, Paris, 1897.

778. PFEIFFER, Ida
      A Lady's Second Journey Around the World...
      [Panama, Peru, Ecuador, etc.]. New York:
      Harper and Brothers, 1852. 302p.; London edi-
      tion, 1855. 2 volumes. (translated from Ger-
      man.)

779. PHILALETHES, Demoticus (pseud.)
      Yankee Travels Through the Island of Cuba
      [description]. New York: D. Appleton and Co.,
      1856. ix, 412p.

780. (PHILIPS, George?)
      Travels in North America [Veracruz and West
      Indies; about 1820]. Dublin: C. Bentham, 1822.
      184p.

781. PHILLIPPO, Rev. James Mursell (1798-1879)
      Jamaica: Its Past and Present State [20 years
      residence by Baptist missionary]. London: J.
      Snow, 1843. xvi, 487p. (Reprinted: Westport,
      Negro Universities Press, 1971; Freeport, Books
      for Libraries, 1971.)

782. PHILLIPPO, Rev. James Mursell
      The United States and Cuba [travel and description].
      New York: Sheldon, Blackman and Co., 1857.
      xi, 476p.

783. PIKE, Zebulon Montgomery (1779-1813)
      An Account of the Expedition to the Sources of
      the Mississippi... [1805-7, including north Mexico].
      Philadelphia: C. and A. Conrad and Co., 1810.
      277p.

784. (PILLING, W.) (pseud: "An Estanciero")
      Ponce de Leon. The Rise of the Argentine Re-
      public [history and description]. Buenos Aires:
      Publisher unknown, 1878. x, 455p.

785. PIM, Bedford Clapperton Travelyan (1826-86) and
      Berthold Carl Seeman (1825-71)
      Dottings on the Roadside in Panama, Nicaragua,
      and Mosquito. London: Chapman and Hill, 1869.
      xvi, 468p.

786. PIM, Bedford Clapperton Trevelyan
      The Gate of the Pacific [Nicaragua].   London:
      Lovell, Reeve and Co., 1863.   viii, 432p.

787. PINCKARD, George (1768-1835)
      Notes on the West Indies [and South America].
      London: Longman, Hunt, Rees and Orme, 1806.
      3 volumes.   (Reprinted: Westport, Greenwood
      Press, 1970.)

788. (POCOCK, Capt.)
      Journal of a Soldier of the 71st or Glasgow Regi-
      ment, 1806-15 [attack on Buenos Aires].   Edin-
      burgh: W. and C. Tait, 1819 (2nd edition) 232p.

789. POINSETTE, Joel Roberts (1779-1851)
      Notes on Mexico Made in the Autumn of 1822...
      [as representative of the United States].   Phila-
      delphia: H. C. Carey and I. Lea, 1824.   viii,
      359p.   (Reprinted: New York, Praeger, 1969.)

790. PONS, François Raymond Joseph de (1751-1812)
      Travels in Parts of South America During the
      Years 1801, 1802, 1803, and 1804 [Venezuela].
      New York: I. Riley, 1806.   3 volumes; various
      editions and titles, New York, London.   (Reprinted:
      New York, A. M. S. Press, 1970.   2 volumes.
      lii, 503, x, 384p.)

791. POOLE, Mrs. Annie Sampson
      Mexicans at Home in the Interior.   London:
      Chapman and Hall, 1884.   viii, 183p.

792. POPHAM, Sir Home Riggs (1762-1820)
      A Full and Correct Report of the Trial of...
      [attack on Buenos Aires, etc.].   London: J. and
      J. Richardson, 1807.   xxxii, 224p.

793. PORTER, Capt. David (1780-1843)
      Journal of a Cruise Made to the Pacific Ocean
      [Argentina, Chile, Peru, Brazil, 1812-1814, by
      United States Noval Officer].   Philadelphia: Brad-
      ford and Inskeep, 1815.   2 volumes.   viii, 263,
      169p.

794. PORTER, Capt. David
      A Voyage to the South Seas in the Years 1812,

1813, and 1814... [Pacific coast of South America].
London: Sir R. Phillips, 1823. 126p.; a United
States edition 1822?

795. PORTER, Sir Robert Ker (1777-1842)
      Caracas Diary, 1825-42. A British Diplomat in a
      New-Born Nation. Caracas: Editorial Arte, 1966.
      cxvi, 1305p. (edited by E. Dupouy.)

796. PORTER, Robert Percival (1852-1917)
      Industrial Cuba. New York: G. P. Putnam's
      Sons, 1899. xi, 428p.

797. POSTEL, Karl Anton (pseud. Charles Sealsfield)
      (1793-1864)
      Scenes and Adventures in Central America [and
      south Mexico]. London: W. Blackwood, 1852.
      298p.

798. POWLES, John Diston (1842-1911)
      The Land of the Pink Pearl; or Recollections of
      Life in the Bahamas. London: Sampson Low,
      Marston, Searle and Rivington, 1888. xi, 321p.

799. POWLES, John Diston
      New Granada; Its Internal Resources [for settlers].
      London: A. H. Baily and Co., 1863. 154p.

800. POYER, John
      The History of Barbados... [and description, 1605-
      1801]. London: J. Mawman. xxxvi, 668p. (Re-
      printed: London, Cass, 1971.)

801. "PREMIUM, Barton" (pseud.)
      Eight Years in British Guiana, Being a Journal
      of a Residence in that Province from 1840 to 1848...
      London: Longman, Brown, Green and Longmans,
      1850. 305p. (edited by "his Friend")

802. PRESCOTT, Thomas H. (pseud. for William O.
      Blake)
      The Volume of the World [statistics, etc., for
      all countries]. Columbus, Ohio: The Author?
      1852. 497p.

803. PRICE, Sir Rose Lambert (1837-99)
      The Two Americas; An Account of Sport and Travel

with Notes on Men and Manners in North and
South America [1874-]. Philadelphia: J. B.
Lippincott and Co. , 1877. viii, 368p. ; also
London, 1877.

804. PRICE, Thomas W.
Brief Notes Taken on a Trip to the City of Mexico in 1878. N. P. Privately printed, 1878?
100p.

805. PRICHARD, Hesketh Vernon (1876-1922)
Through the Heart of Patagonia [end of century].
New York: D. Appleton and Co. , 1902. xvi,
346p. ; also London, 1902.

806. PRICHARD, Hesketh Vernon
Where Black Rules White, a Journey Across and
About Haiti [before 1900]. Westminster: Archi-
bald Constable and Co. , 1900. 288p.

807. PROCTOR, Robert
Narrative of a Journey Across the Cordillera of
the Andes, and Residence in Lima and Other Parts
of Peru, 1823-24 [Peru, Chile, Argentina]. London: Archibald Constable and Co. , 1825. xx,
374p.

Q

808. QUESADA, Gonzalo de (1868-1915)
America's Battle for Cuba's Freedom [description,
etc.]. Philadelphia: National Publishing Co. ,
1898. 768p.

809. QUESADA, Gonzalo de and Henry Davenport Northrop
(1836-1909)
Cuba's Great Struggle for Freedom [history and
description]. Washington: Library of Congress,
1898. 725p.

810. QUESADA, Gonzalo de and Henry Davenport Northrop
The War in Cuba [history and description]. Boston: Liberty Publishing Co. , 1896. 592p. (Reprinted: New York, Arno Press, 1970.)

R

811.   RAFTER, Col. M.
       Memoirs of Gregor McGregor [patriot activities;
       Miranda, Bolívar, etc.]. London: J. J. Stockdale,
       1820. 426p.

812.   RAINSFORD, Capt. Marcus
       An Historical Account of the Black Empire of Hayti
       [and description by British officer]. London: J.
       Cundee, 1805. xxiv, 467p.

813.   RAMPINI, Charles Joseph Galliari (b. 1840)
       Letters from Jamaica. Edinburgh: Edmonton
       and Douglas, 1873. 182p.

814.   RANKIN, Malinda
       Twenty Years Among the Mexicans. A Narrative
       of Missionary Labor. Cincinnati: Chase and Hall,
       1871. 214p.

815.   RANYARD, Mrs. Ellen Henrietta (pseud: L. N. R.)
       (1810-79) (editor)
       The Book and its Mission; Past and Present
       [articles and reports of members of the British
       and Foreign Bible Society on South America].
       Philadelphia: Parry and McMillan, 1854. xiv,
       508p.; also London, 6 parts, 1856-59.

816.   RAY, G. Whitfield
       Through Five Republics on Horseback. Being an
       Account of Many Wanderings in South America
       [Argentina, Uruguay, Paraguay, Brazil, Bolivia,
       1889-]. Toronto: W. Briggs, 1911. 381p.
       (5th edition)

817.   REA, George Bronson (1869-1936)
       Facts and Fakes about Cuba [circulated in the
       United States]. New York: George Munro's Sons,
       1897. 336p.

818.   RECLUS, Jean Jacques Elisée (1830-1906)
       The Earth and Its Inhabitants [Vol. 17, Mexico and
       Central America; Vol. 18, South America and the
       Andes; Vol. 19, Amazon and La Plata. Descrip-
       tion, geography, etc.]. London: J. S. Virtue and
       Co., 1876-94. 19 volumes.

819. REDPATH, James (1833-91) (editor)
      A Guide to Haiti. Boston: Thayer and Eldridge,
      1860. 180p. (Reprinted: Westport, Negro
      Universities Press, 1971.)

820. REID, Samuel Chester (1818-97)
      The Scouting Expedition of McCulloch's Texas
      Rangers [campaigns; land and people of Mexico in
      1846]. Philadelphia: G. B. Zeiber and Co., 1847.
      251p.

821. REISS, Johann Wilhelm (1838-1908) and Alphons
      Stübel (1835-1904)
          The Necropolis of Ancón in Peru [description].
          Berlin: Asher and Co., 1880-87. 3 volumes.
          (translated from German.)

822. RENGGER, Johann Rudolph (1795-1832) and Marçel
      François Xavier Lonchamps
          The Reign of Dr. Gaspard Rodrick de Francia in
          Paraguay. Six Years in that Republic [1819-25].
          London: T. Hurst, E. Chance, 1827. xvi, 208p.
          (translated from French.) (Reprinted: Port
          Washington, Kennikat, 1971.)

823. RENNY, Robert
          A History of Jamaica [and description]. London:
          J. Cawthorn, 1807. xx, 333p.

824. "A RESIDENT" (pseud. for J. H. Kerr or "Miss Browne")
          Sketches and Recollections of the West Indies.
          London: Smith, Elder and Co., 1828. 330p.

825. RESTREPO, Vicente
          A Study of the Gold and Silver Mines of Colombia
          [history, description]. New York: Colombian Con-
          sulate, 1886. 320p. (translated from Spanish.)

826. REVILLE, Albert (1826-1906)
          The Native Religions of Mexico and Peru [history
          and description]. New York: Charles Scribner's
          Sons, 1884. x, 213p.

827. REVY, Julian John
          Hydraulics of Great Rivers: The Paraná, the
          Uruguay and the La Plata Estuary. New York:
          E. and F. Spon, 1874. xvi, 163p.; also London
          edition, 1874.

828.   REYNOLDS, Jeremiah N. (1799-1858)
       Voyage of the United States Frigate Patomic...
       [around the world, Rio de Janeiro, and west coast
       ports, 1831-4]. New York: Harper and Brothers,
       1835. 500p. (a shorter first edition, 1834?)

829.   RHODES, James A.
       A Cruise in a Whale Boat ... Reminiscences and
       Adventures During a Year in the Pacific Ocean
       and the Interior of South America. New York:
       New York Publishing Co., 1848. 107p.

830.   RICE, John J.
       Mexico, Our Neighbor. New York: Levell, 1888.
       124p.

831.   RICKARD, Maj. Francis Ignacio
       The Mineral and other Resources of the Argentine
       Republic in 1869. London: Longmans, Green and
       Co., 1870. 323p.

832.   RICKARD, Maj. Francis Ignacio
       A Mining Journey Across the Great Andes [Chile,
       Argentina, 1862-3]. London: Smith, Elder and
       Co., 1863. xvi, 314p.

833.   RIEDEL, Emil
       Practical Guide to the City and Valley of Mexico.
       Mexico City: I. Epstein, 1892. 427p.

834.   RILAND, Rev. John (1778-1863) (editor)
       Memoirs of a West Indian Planter [about 1801-21;
       writer unknown]. London: Hamilton, Adams and
       Co., 1827. xxxv, 218p.

835.   RIPLEY, Mrs. Eliza Moore (Chinn) McHatton (1832-
       1912)
       From Flag to Flag. A Woman's Adventures and
       Experiences in the South During the War in Mexico
       and in Cuba. New York: Appleton and Co., 1889.
       296p.

836.   RIVERO y Ustáriz, Mariano Eduardo (1798?-1857)
       and Johann Jakob Von Tschudi (1818-89)
       Peruvian Antiquities [history and description].
       New York: G. P. Putnam, 1853. xxii, 306p.;

first published, Vienna, 1851. (translated from
Spanish.) (Reprinted: New York, Kraus, 1971,
from 1855 edition.)

837. ROBERTS, Edwards
With the Invader; Glimpses of the Southwest [and
Mexico]. San Francisco: S. Carson and Co.,
1885. 156p.

838. ROBERTS, Orlando W.
Narrative of Voyages and Excursions on the East
Coast and in the Interior of Central America [a
resident trader's experiences]. Edinburgh: Constable and Sons, 1827. 302p. (Reprinted: Gainesville, University of Florida Press, 1865.)

839. (ROBERTSON, John Blount)
Reminiscences of a Campaign in Mexico [Mexican
War; description of people and places]. Nashville:
J. York and Co., 1849. 288p.

840. ROBERTSON, John Parish (1792-1843) and William
Parish Robertson
Letters on Paraguay; Comprising an Account of
Four Years' Residence in that Republic under the
Government of the Dictator Francia. London:
John Murray, 1838-39. 3 volumes. xxvii, 359,
x, 342, xvi, 400p. (several other editions with
other titles.)

841. ROBERTSON, John Parish and William Parish
Robertson
Letters on South America, Comprising Travels on
the Banks of the Paraná and the Río de la Plata.
London: John Murray, 1843. 3 volumes. xi, iv,
320, ix, 300, vii, 345p. (Reprinted: New York,
A.M.S. Press, 1970.)

842. ROBERTSON, Thomas A.
A Southwestern Utopia [Mexico, 1886-95]. Los
Angeles: The Ward Ritchie Press, 1947. ?p.
(first edition?)

843. ROBERTSON, William Parish
A Visit to Mexico by the West Indian Islands,
Yucatan and the United States. London: Simpkin,
Marshall and Co., 1853. 2 volumes.

844. ROBESON, George Maxwell (1827-97)
      Reports of Explorations and Surveys for the Loca-
      tion of a Ship-Canal Between the Atlantic and
      Pacific Oceans Through Nicaragua, 1872-3.   Wash-
      ington: Government Printing Office, 1874.   ?p.

845. ROBINSON, Alfred (1807-95) (and Friar Geronimo
      Boscana)
      Life in California, During a Residence of Several
      Years in that Territory [Mexican California, 1829-
      46]. New York: Wiley and Putnam, 1846.   341p.
      (Reprinted: New York, Da Capo Press, 1969;
      Santa Barbara, Peregrine Press, 1971.)

846. ROBINSON, James H.
      Journal of an Expedition 1400 Miles up the
      Orinoco and 300 up the Arauca....   London:
      Black, Young and Young, 1822.   xix, 397p.

847. ROBINSON, Tracy (1833-1915)
      Fifty Years at Panama [1861-   ].   (title varies)
      New York: Star and Herald Co. , 1907.   xiii,
      282p.

848. ROBINSON, William Davis
      Memoirs of the Mexican Revolution, Including a
      Narrative of the Expedition of General Xavier
      Mina, and Some Observations on the Practicability
      of Opening a Commerce Between the Pacific and
      Atlantic Oceans [Mexico, Nicaragua].   Philadelphia:
      The Author, 1820.   2 volumes.   li, 328, vii,
      389p.

849. ROBINSON, Wirt
      A Flying Trip to the Tropics [ornithological trip
      to Colombia, Curaçao, West Indies, 1892].   Cam-
      bridge: Riverside Press, 1895.   x, 194p.

850. RODENBOUGH, Theophilus Francis (1838-1919)
      (editor)
      From Everglades to Canyon with the Second
      Dragoons [Florida, Mexico, western United States].
      New York: D. Van Nostrand, 1875.   561p.

851. RODNEY, Caesar Agustus (1772-1824) and John
      Graham (1774-1820)
      The Reports on the Present State of the United

Provinces of South America [1817-18].   London:
Baldwin, Cradock and Joy, 1819.   viii, 358p.
(Reprinted: New York, Praeger, 1969.)

852. RODRIGUES, José Carlos (1844-1922)
The Panama Canal; its History, its Political
Aspects and Financial Difficulties.   New York:
Charles Scribner's Sons, 1885.   viii, 248p.;
also London edition, 1885.

853. RODWAY, James (1848-1926)
In the Guiana Forest.   Studies of Nature in Rela-
tion to the Struggle for Life [British Guiana].
New York: Charles Scribner's Sons, 1894.   xxiii,
242p. (Reprinted: Westport, Negro Universities
Press, 1971.)

854. RODWAY, James
In the Guiana Wilds.   A Study of Two Women.
Boston: L. C. Page and Co., 1899.   270p.

855. RODWAY, James
The West Indies and the Spanish Main.   London:
T. Fisher Unwin, 1896.   xxiv, 371p. (Reprinted:
Westport, Negro Universities Press, 1971.)

856. ROGERS, Carlton H.
Incidents of Travel in the Southern States and
Cuba.   New York: R. Craighead, 1852.   320p.

857. ROGERS, Thomas L.
Mexico? Si Señor.   Boston: Collins Press, 1893.
294p.

858. ROLPH, Dr. Thomas (1820?-83)
A Brief Account, Together with Observations,
Made During a Visit to the West Indies [and the
United States and Canada].   Dundas, Upper
Canada: G. H. Hackstaff, 1836.   242, +16p.

859. ROMERO, José
Diaries and Accounts of the Romero Expeditions in
Arizona and California, 1823-26 [North Mexico].
Los Angeles: Ward Ritchie Press, 1962.   xvii,
117p. (edited by L. J. Bean and William Mason.)

860.   ROMERO, Matías (1837-98)
        Geographical and Statistical Notes on Mexico.
        New York: G. P. Putnam's Sons, 1898.   xvi,
        286p.   (translated from Spanish.)

861.   ROSS, Sir James Clark (1800-62)
        A Voyage of Discovery and Research in the South-
        ern and Antarctic Regions, During the Years 1839
        to 1843 [South America].   London: John Murray,
        1847.   2 volumes.   liv, 355, xiv, 447p.   (Re-
        printed: New York, A. M. Kelley, 1969.)

862.   ROTHERY, Lt. G. A.
        A Diary of the Wreck of His Majesty's Ship
        Challenger on the Western Coast of South America
        [Chile, May, 1835].   London: Longman, Rees,
        Orme, Brown, Green and Longmans, 1836.   160p.

863.   ROUGHLEY, Thomas
        The Jamaica Planter's Guide; or a System of Plant-
        ing and Managing a Sugar Estate... [twenty years
        in British West Indies].   London: Longman, Hurst,
        Rees, Orme and Brown, 1823.   x, 420p.

864.   ROWAN, Andrew Summers (b. 1857) and Marathon
        Montrose Ramsey
        The Island of Cuba.   A Descriptive and Historical
        Account....   New York: Henry Holt, 1896.   x,
        279p.

865.   RUMBOLD, Sir Horace (1829-1813)
        The Great Silver River.   Notes of a Residence in
        Buenos Aires in 1880 and 1881.   London: John
        Murray, 1887.   14, +366p.

866.   RUSCHENBERGER, William Samuel Waitman (1807-95)
        Three Years in the Pacific [United States naval
        officer on West coast of South America and Brazil,
        1826-29, 1831-4].   Philadelphia: Carey, Lea,
        and Blanchard, 1834.   xi, 441p.

867.   RUSSELL, Sir William Howard (1820-1907)
        A Visit to Chile and the Nitrate Fields of
        Tarapacá... [by a war correspondent, 1841-63].
        London: J. S. Virtue, 1890.   xii, 374p.

868. RUXTON, George Frederick Augustus (1820-48)
Adventures in Mexico. From Vera Cruz to
Chihuahua in the Days of the Mexican War. New
York: Harper and Brothers, 1847. 168p.
London edition, 1847.

869. RYAN, William Redmond (1791-1855)
Personal Adventures in Upper and Lower California in 1848-49. London: W. Shoberl, 1850.
2 volumes.

S

870. SACK, Albert (Baron von)
A Narrative of a Voyage to Surinam [and residence, 1805-7]. London: G. and W. Nicol, 1810.
x, 282p.

871. ST. CLAIR, Thomas Stanton
A Residence in the West Indies and America [also
titled A Soldier's Recollections...]. London:
Robert Bentley, 1834. 2 volumes. xiv, 395, xii,
382p.

872. ST. JOHN, Sir Spencer Buckingham (1825-1910)
Hayti or the Black Republic [20 years residence].
London: Smith, Elder and Co., 1884. xiv, 343p.;
revised, enlarged, London, 1889. (Reprinted:
London, Cass, 1971.)

873. SALA, George Augustus Henry (1828-95)
Under the Sun [Cuba, etc.]. London: Tinsley
Brothers, 1872. xix, 395p.

874. SALM-SALM, Agnes Inés
Ten Years of My Life [attempt to release Maximilian in Mexico]. London: R. Bentley? 1875.
2 volumes.

875. SALM-SALM, Prince Felix zu
My Diary in Mexico in 1867, Including the Last
Days of the Emperor Maximilian. London: R.
Bentley, 1868. 2 volumes.

876. SALMON, Charles Spencer
The Caribbean Confederation. A Plan for the

Union of the Fifteen British West Indian Colonies....
London: Cassell and Co., 1888. 175p. (Reprinted: Westport, Negro Universities Press,
1971.)

877. SALVIN, Rev. Hugh S. (1773-1852)
      Journal Written on Board His Majesty's Ship
      Cambridge [South America, 1824-7]. Newcastle:
      Edward Walker, 1829. 245p.

878. SANBORN, Helen Josephine (1857-1917)
      A Winter in Central America and Mexico. Boston:
      Lee and Shepard, 1886. iv, 321p.; also New York:
      C. T. Dillingham, 1886.

879. SANTA Anna, Antonio López de (1795-1876)
      The Eagle. The Autobiography of... [1810-74].
      Austin: The Pemberton Press, 1967. xx, 299p.
      (Edited by Ann Fears Crawford.)

880. SANTA-Anna Nery, Frederico José de (Baron) (1849-
      1902)
      The Land of the Amazons [1880s?]. London:
      Sands and Co., 1901. xlii, 405p.; first edition,
      Paris, 1884? (Translated from French.)

881. SARMIENTO, Domingo Faustino (1811-88)
      Life in the Argentine Republic in the Days of the
      Tyrants.... New York: Hurd and Houghton,
      1868. xxxv, 400p. (Translated from Spanish.)

882. SARTORIUS, Carl Christian Wilhelm (1796-1872)
      Mexico. Landscapes and Popular Sketches. New
      York: Lange and Kronfeld, 1858? vi, 202p.
      (Translated from German.)

883. SAUNDERS, Prince (editor) (1755-1839)
      Haytian Papers [official papers, documents,
      description, etc., 1804-14]. London: W. Reed,
      1816. xv, 228p. (Reprinted: Westport, Green-
      wood, 1971.)

884. SAVAGE, Charles C.
      The World. Geographical, Historical and Statis-
      tical [North and South America, etc.]. New York:
      Phelps, 1853. 496p.

885. SCARLETT, Peter Campbell (1804-81)
      South America and the Pacific [Buenos Aires,
      Rio de Janeiro, Valparaiso, Lima, Panama].
      London: H. Colburn, 1838. 2 volumes. xii,
      314, viii, 352p.

886. SCHAEFFER, Luther Melancthon
      Sketches of Travels in South America, Mexico
      and California. New York: James Egbert, 1860.
      247p.

887. SCHERZER, Karl von (1821-1903) and Moritz Wagner
      Travels in the Free States of Central America
      [Nicaragua, Honduras, El Salvador]. London:
      Longman, Brown, Green, Longmans and Roberts,
      1857. 2 volumes. xvi, 320, xii, 253p. (trans-
      lated from German.) (Reprinted: New York,
      A. M. S. Press, 1970.)

888. SCHMIDTMEYER, Peter
      Travels into Chile over the Andes in the Years
      1820 and 1821. London: Longman, Hurst, Rees,
      Orme, Brown, Green, 1824. 379p.

889. SCHOMBURGK, Sir Robert Hermann (1804-65)
      A Description of British Guiana. London: Simp-
      kin, Marshall and Co., 1840. 155p. (Reprinted:
      Clifton, N. J., A. M. Kelley, 1970.)

890. SCHOMBURGK, Sir Robert Hermann
      The History of the Barbados... [and description].
      London: Longman, Brown, Green and Longmans,
      1848. xx, 722p. (Reprinted: Clifton, N. J.,
      A. M. Kelley, 1971.)

891. SCHOMBURGK, Sir Robert Hermann
      The Natural History of the Fishes of Guiana.
      Edinburgh: W. H. Lizars, 1841-3. 2 volumes.

892. SCHOMBURGK, Sir Robert Hermann
      Travels in British Guiana, 1840-44. Leipzig:
      J. J. Webber, 1847. 2 volumes. xxxviii, 402,
      xii, 443p.

893. SCHROEDER, Seaton (1849-1922)
      The Fall of Maximilian's Empire as Seen from

a United States Gun-Boat [1867]. New York:
G. P. Putnam's Sons, 1887. vi, 130p.

894. SCHWATKA, Lt. Frederick (1849-92)
      In the Land of Cave and Cliff Dwellers [Mexico].
      Boston: Educational Publishing Co. , 1889. vi,
      385p.

895. SCLATER, Philip Lutley (1829-1913) and William
      Henry Hudson (1841-1922)
      Argentine Ornithology. A Descriptive Catalogue
      of the Birds of the Argentine Republic. London:
      R. H. Porter, 1888-89. 2 volumes.

896. SCOTT, General Winfield (1786-1866)
      Memoirs [War with Mexico, etc.]. New York:
      Sheldon, 1864. 2 volumes.

897. SCRUGGS, William Lindsay (1836-1912)
      The Colombian and Venezuelan Republics... [his-
      tory and description, 1872-99]. Boston: Little,
      Brown, 1900. xii, 350p.; also a London edition,
      1900.

898. SCULLY, William (editor)
      Brazil; its Provinces and Chief Cities [a guide].
      London: John Murray, 1866. xvi, 398p.

899. SEALSFIELD, Charles (pseud. for Karl Anton Postel)
      (1793-1864)
      North and South; or Scenes and Adventures in
      Mexico. New York: J. Einchester, 1844. 118p.
      (translated from German.)

900. SEAMAN, Elizabeth Cochrane (1867-1922)
      Six Months in Mexico. New York: American
      Publisher's Corporation, 1888. 205p.

901. SEEBEE, Felix
      Travelling Impressions in, and Notes on, Peru
      [1880-81]. London: Elliot Stock, 1901. 196p.

902. SELER, Edward (1849-1922)
      Mexico and Guatemala. Berlin: Reimer, 1896.
      iv, 267p. (translated from German.)

903. SELFRIDGE, Commador Thomas Oliver
      Reports of Explorations and Surveys to Ascertain
      the Practicability of a Ship Canal Between the
      Atlantic and Pacific Oceans by Way of the Isthmus
      of Darien [1870-74]. Washington: Government
      Printing Office, 1874. 268p.

904. SELLERIER, Carlos
      Data Referring to Mexican Mining [prepared for
      Paris Exposition, 1900]. Mexico: F. P. Hoeck
      and Co., 1901. 140p.

905. SEMMES, Lt. Raphael (1809-77)
      Service Afloat and Ashore During the Mexican
      War [account by Rear Adm., Confederate Navy].
      Cincinnati: W. H. Moon and Co., 1851. 480p.

906. SEMPLE, Robert (1766-1816)
      Sketch of the Present State of Caracas; including
      a Journey from Caracas Through La Victoria and
      Valencia to Porto Cabello. London: Robert Bald-
      win, 1812. viii, 176p.

907. SENIOR, Bernard Martin (pseud: "Retired Military
      Officer")
      Jamaica as it was, as it is, and as it will be....
      London: T. Hurst, 1835. vii, 312p. (Reprinted:
      Westport, Negro Universities Press, 1971.)

908. SEWELL, William Grant (1829-62)
      The Ordeal of Free Labor in the British West
      Indies [letters]. New York: Harper and Brothers,
      1861. vi, 325p. (Reprinted: New York, A. M.
      Kelley, 1968.)

909. SEYMOUR, Richard Arthur
      Pioneering in the Pampas, or the First Four
      Years of a Settler's Experience in the La Plata
      Camps [1865-]. London: Longmans, Green and
      Co., 1869. xii, 180p.

910. SHAW, Arthur E.
      Forty Years in the Argentine Republic [1864-].
      London: Elkin Mathews, 1907. 229p.

911. SHELDEN, Henry Isaac
      Notes on the Nicaraguan Canal. Chicago: A. C.
      McClurg, 1897. 214p.

912. SHEPARD, Ashbel K.
      The Land of the Aztecs, or Two Years in Mexico.
      Albany: Weed Parsons and Co., 1859.   209p.

913. SHEPHARD, Charles
      Historical Account of the Island of St. Vincent
      [and description]. London: W. Nicol, 1831.   xix,
      216p.

914. SHEPHERD, Grant (1875-1939)
      The Silver Magnet. Fifty Years in a Mexican
      Silver Mine [in Chihuahua]. New York: E. P.
      Dutton, 1938. 302p.

915. (SHERMAN, John H.)
      A General Account of Miranda's Expedition [an
      officer's adventures]. New York: McFarlane
      and Long, 1808. 120p.

916. SHERRATT, Harriot Wight
      Mexican Vistas seen from Highways and Byways
      of Travel. Chicago: Rand, McNally and Co.,
      1899. 285p.

917. SCHILLIBEER, Lt. John
      A Narrative of the Britain's Voyage to Pitcairns
      Island [and South America: Brazil, Chile, Peru].
      London: Law and Whittaker, 1817. iii, 179p.

918. SHOEMAKER, Michael Myers (1853-1824)
      The Kingdom of the "White Woman." A Sketch
      [Mexico]. Cincinnati: Robert Clarke Co., 1894.
      207p.

919. SHUFELDT, Robert Wilson (1822-95)
      Report of Explorations and Surveys to Ascertain
      the Practicability of a Ship-Canal Between Atlantic
      and Pacific Oceans, by Way of the Isthmus of
      Tehuantepec. Washington: Government Printing
      Office, 1872. 151p.

920. SIDNEY, Henry
      The Travels and Extraordinary Adventures of
      Henry Sidney in Brazil in the Years 1809, 1810,
      1811 and 1812. London: J. Ferguson, 1815.
      iv, 159p.

921. SIGSBEE, Capt. Charles Dwight
The "Maine"; an Account of her Destruction in
Havana Harbor... [incidents and description].
New York: Century Co., 1899. xiv, 270p.; also
London, 1899.

922. SIMMONS, William E.
Uncle Sam's New Waterway [Nicaragua Canal].
New York: F. T. Neely, 1899. 285p.; new
edition and title, New York: Harper, 1900.

923. SIMMS, William Gilmore (1806-70)
Southward Ho. A Spell of Sunshine. New York:
Redfield, 1854. 472p. (Reprinted: New York,
A. M. S. Press, 1970.)

924. SIMSON, Alfred
Travels in the Wilds of Ecuador and the Exploration of the Putumayo River [1877?]. London:
Simpson Low, Marston, Searle and Rivington, 1886.
vi, 270p.

925. SINCLAIR, Arthur
In Tropical Lands: Recent Travels to the Sources
of the Amazon, the West Indian Islands and Ceylon.
Aberdeen: D. Wyllie, 1895. 193p.

926. (SKINNER, Capt. Joseph) (editor)
The Present State of Peru.... London: R.
Phillips, 1805. xiv, 487p. (translated from
Spanish.)

927. SMITH, Mrs. Ann Eliza Brainerd (pseud: "Mrs. J. G.
Smith") (1818-1905)
Notes of Travel in Mexico and California. St. Al-
bans, Vt.: Messinger and Advertiser, 1886. 123p.

928. SMITH, Dr. Archibald (d. 1868)
Peru as it is. Comprising an Account of the
Social and Physical Features of the Country. London: Richard Bentley, 1839. 2 volumes. xi,
299, v, 308p.

929. SMITH, Edmond Reuel
The Araucanians, or Notes of a Tour Among the
Indian Tribes of Southern Chile [1849-52]. New
York: Harper and Brothers, 1855. xii, 335p.

930. SMITH, Francis Hopkinson (1838-1915)
      A White Unbrellow in Mexico. Boston: Houghton
      Mifflin, 1889. viii, 227p.

931. SMITH, Herbert Huntington (1851-1919)
      Brazil; the Amazon and the Coast [1870 and 1874].
      New York: Charles Scribners, 1879. xvi, 644p.

932. SMITH, Moses
      History of the Adventures and Sufferings of...
      [with Miranda, 1806-11]. Brooklyn: Thomas
      Kirk, 1812. 124p.

933. SMITH, William Anderson (b. 1842)
      Temperate Chile: A Progressive Spain. London:
      Adam and Charles Black, 1899. x, 399p.

934. SMITH, W. F.
      Guide to Havana, Mexico and New York [description
      of principal cities in Cuba and Mexico]. New
      York: W. F. Smith Co., 1885. ?p.

935. SMYTH, William (1800-77) and Frederick Lowe
      Narrative of a Journey from Lima to Pará...
      [1824-35]. London: John Murray, 1836. vii,
      305p.

936. SNOW, William Parker (1817-95)
      Two Years' Cruise off Tierra del Fuego, the
      Falkland Islands, Patagonia and the River Plate.
      London: Longman, Brown, Green, Longmans
      and Roberts, 1857. 2 volumes. xv, 376, viii,
      368p.

937. SOLTERA, Maria (pseud. for Mary Lester)
      A Lady's Ride Across Spanish Honduras. London:
      Blackwood's Magazine, 1884. vi, 319p. (Re-
      printed: Gainesville, University of Florida Press,
      1964.)

938. SORTORIOUS, Carl Christain Wilhelm (1796-1872)
      Mexican Landscapes and Popular Sketches [about
      1850]. Darmstadt: G. G. Lange, 1858. viii,
      202p.

939. SOUTHEY, Robert (1774-1843)
      History of Brazil [to about 1812; descriptions and

observations]. London: Longman, Hurst, Rees,
Orme and Brown, 1810-19. 3 volumes. xxxiv,
715, xliii, xvi, 718, xx, 959p. (Reprinted:
New York, Burt Franklin, 1971; and Westport,
Greenwood, 1971.)

940. SOUTHEY, Robert
A Tale of Paraguay [poem]. London: Longman,
Hurst, Rees, Orme, Brown and Green, 1825.
xviii, 199p.

941. SOUTHEY, Capt. Thomas
Chronological History of the West Indies [and
description by British naval officer]. London:
Longman, Rees, Orme, Brown and Green, 1827.
3 volumes. viii, 336, vi, 552, iv, 620p. (Reprinted: New York, Barnes and Noble, 1968.)

942. SPEARS, John Randolph (1850-1936)
The Gold Diggings of Cape Horn. A Study of
Life in Tierra del Fuego and Patagonia. New
York: G. P. Putnam's Sons, 1895. xi, 319p.

943. SPENCE, James Mudie
The Land of Bolívar, or War, Peace and Adventure in the Republic of Venezuela. London: Sampson Low, Marston, Searle and Rivington, 1878.
2 volumes. x, 323, xii, 345p. (Reprinted: New
York, A. M. S. Press, 1969.)

944. SPIX, Johann Baptist von (1781-1826) and Carl
Friedrich Philipp von Martius (1704-1868)
Travels in Brazil [1817-20]. London: Longman,
Hurst, Rees, Orme, Brown and Green, 1824.
2 volumes. (translated from German.)

945. SPRUCE, Richard (1817-93)
Notes of a Botanist on the Amazon and Andes
[1849-54]. London: Reeve and Co., 1852-53.
2 volumes. (edited by Alfred Russell Wallace.)

946. SQUIER, Ephriam George (1821-88)
Honduras. Descriptive, Historical and Statistical.
London: Trübner and Co., 1870. viii, 278p.
(Reprinted: New York, A. M. S. Press, 1969.)

947.   SQUIER, Ephraim George
       Honduras Interocean Railway.   London: Trübner
       and Co. , 1857.   xvi, 100p.

948.   SQUIER, Ephraim George
       Nicaragua.   Its People, Scenery Monuments and
       the Proposed Interoceanic Canal. ...   New York:
       D. Appleton, 1852.   2 volumes.   xxiv, 424, iv,
       452p.   (same as Travels in Central America... ,
       New York, Harpers, 1853.)   (Reprinted: New
       York, Johnson, 1968; New York, A. M. S. Press,
       1969.)

949.   SQUIER, Ephriam George
       Notes on Central America, Particularly the States
       of Honduras and San Salvador... [and Honduras
       inter-ocean railroad].   New York: Harper and
       Brothers, 1855.   397p.   (Reprinted: New York,
       Praeger, 1969; and New York, A. M. S. Press,
       1969.)

950.   SQUIER, Ephraim George
       Peru.   Incidents of Travel and Exploration in the
       Land of the Incas.   New York: Hurst and Co. ,
       1877.   xx, 599p.; also London: Macmillan, 1877.
       (Reprinted: New York, Johnson, 1968; New York,
       A. M. S.   Press, 1969.)

951.   SQUIER, Ephraim George
       The States of Central America.   Their Geography,
       Topography and Climate. ...   New York: Hurst
       and Co. , 1858.   782p.

952.   SQUIER, Ephraim George (pseud: S. A. Bard)
       Waikna.   Adventures on the Mosquita Shore
       [British Honduras; fiction].   New York: Harper
       and Brothers, 1855.   366p.   (Reprinted: Gaines-
       ville, University of Florida Press, 1965.)

953.   STANLEY, Edward Henry Smith (15th Earl of Derby)
       Six Weeks in South America [Ecuador, Colombia,
       Peru].   London: T. and W. Boone, 1850.   iv,
       132p.

954.   STAPP, William Preston
       The Prisoners of Perote, Containing a Journal

Kept by the Author who was Captured by the
Mexicans at Mier... [1842-44]. Philadelphia:
G. B. Zieber and Co., 1845. 164p.

955. STARK, James Henry
       Stark's History and Guide to the Bahama Islands.
       Boston: J. H. Stark, 1891. x, 243p.

956. STARK, James Henry
       Stark's Illustrated Bermuda Guide. Boston:
       Photo-Electrotype Co., 1888. 192p.

957. STARK, James Henry
       Stark's Jamaica Guide.... Boston: J. H. Stark,
       1898. viii, 207p.

958. STEELE, James William (1840-1905)
       Cuban Sketches. New York: G. P. Putnam's
       Sons, 1881. vii, 220p.

959. STEPHEN, Sir George
       Anti-Slavery Recollections [letters to Mrs.
       Beecher Stowe on West Indian slavery]. London:
       Thomas Hatchard, 1854. xxxii, 258p.

960. STEPHEN, James (1758-1832)
       Bonaparte in the West: or the History of Tous-
       saint Louverture, the African Hero [Toussaint,
       1746?-1803; history and description of Haiti].
       London: J. Hatchard, 1803. 3 volumes.

961. STEPHEN, James
       The Crisis of the Sugar Colonies [British West
       Indies]. London: J. Hatchard, 1808? vii, 222p.
       (Reprinted: Westport, Negro Universities Press,
       1971.)

962. STEPHEN, James
       The Slavery of the British West India Colonies
       Delineated. London: J. Butterworth, 1824-30.
       2 volumes. lxxi, 480, xliv, 452p.

963. STEPHENS, Charles Asbury (1845-1931)
       The Knockabout Club in the Tropics. Adventures
       of a Party of Youth in New Mexico, Mexico and
       Central America. Boston: Estes and Lauriat,
       1883. 240p.

964.   STEPHENS, John Lloyd (1805-52)
        Incidents of Travel in Central America, Chiapas
        and Yucatan [1839-40].   New York: R.I. Pred-
        nore, 1841-2.   2 volumes.   (Reprinted: New
        York, Dover, 1969; Norman, University of Okla-
        homa Press, 1962.)

965.   STEPHENS, John Lloyd
        Incidents of Travel in Yucatan.   New York:
        Harper and Brothers, 1843.   2 volumes.   (Re-
        printed: Norman, University of Oklahoma Press,
        1960; New York, Dover, 1963.)

966.   STERNE, Henry (b. 1801)
        A Statement of Fact... [system of Jamaican ap-
        prenticeship].   London: J.C. Chappell, 1837.
        xii, 282p.

967.   STEUART, John
        Bogotá in 1836-37.   Being a Narrative of an Ex-
        pedition to the Capital of New Granada and a
        Residence there of 11 months.   New York:
        Harper and Brothers, 1838.   viii, 312p.

968.   STEVENSON, Frederick James (1835-1926)
        A Traveller in the Sixties [diaries and journals;
        Brazil, Argentina, Peru, Chile, Bolivia, 1867-9].
        London: Constable and Co., 1929.   xvi, 308p.
        (edited by Douglas Timins.)

969.   STEVENSON, Paul Eve (1868-1910)
        By Way of Cape Horn.   Four Months in a Yankee
        Clipper.   Philadelphia: J.B. Lippincott, 1899.
        419p.

970.   STEVENSON, Mrs. Sara York (1847-1921)
        Maximilian in Mexico.   A Woman's Reminiscences
        in Mexico of the French Intervention, 1862-1867.
        New York: Century Co., 1899.   xiv, 327p.

971.   STEVENSON, William Bennet (b. 1787?)
        Historical and Descriptive Narrative of Twenty
        Year's Residence in South America [Chile and
        Peru, 1805-25].   London: Hurst, Robinson and
        Co., 1825.   3 volumes.   xii, 439, viii, 434,
        vii, 467p.

972.   STEWART, Rev. Charles Samuel (1795-1870)
       Brazil and La Plata. The Personal Record of a
       Cruise [American missionary in Brazil, Argentina,
       Uruguay, 1850-52]. New York: G. P. Putnam and
       Co., 1856. xii, 428p.

973.   STEWART, Rev. Charles Samuel
       A Visit to the South Seas in the United States
       Ship Vincennes during the Years 1829 and 1830
       [Brazil and Peru]. New York: John P. Haven,
       1831. 2 volumes. xi, 357, iv, 360p.

974.   (STEWART, John) (pseud: "A Gentleman")
       An Account of Jamaica (and its Inhabitants)
       [during 21 years]. London: Longman, Hurst,
       Rees and Orme, 1808. xii, 305p. (Reprinted:
       Freeport, Books for Libraries, 1971.)

975.   STEWART, John
       A View of the Past and Present State of the
       Island of Jamaica.... Edinburgh: Oliver and
       Boyd, 1823. xiii, 363p. (Reprinted: Westport,
       Negro Universities Press, 1969.)

976.   STILLMAN, Jacob Davis Babcock (1819-88)
       Seeking the Golden Fleese [Central America and
       California]. San Francisco: A Roman and Co.,
       1871. 352p.

977.   STODDARD, Charles Augustus (1833-1920)
       Cruising Among the Caribbees. Summer Days in
       Winter Months. New York: Charles Scribner's
       Sons, 1895. xii, 198p.; also London, 1895.

978.   STOUT, Peter F.
       Nicaragua. Past, Present and Future. Phila-
       delphia: John E. Potter and Co., 1859. 372p.

979.   STRAIN, Lt. Isaac G. (1821-57)
       Cordillera and Pampa, Mountain and Plain.
       Sketches of a Journey in Chile and the Argentine
       Provinces in 1849. New York: Horace H. Moore,
       1853. xi, 296p.

908.   STRANGEWAYS, Thomas
       Sketches of the Mosquito Shore, Including the

Territory of Poyais... [for the use of settlers].
Edinburgh: W. Blackwood, 1822. viii, 355p.

981. STREET, George G.
Che! Wah! Wah!, or the Modern Montezumas
in Mexico. Rochester, N.Y.: E.R. Andrews,
1883. 115p.

982. STUART, Henry Winsor Villiers (1827-95)
Adventures Amidst the Equatorial Forests and
Rivers of South America; also in the West Indies
and the Wilds of Florida. London: John Murray, 1891. xxiv, 268p.

983. STURGE, Joseph (1793-1859) and Thomas Harvey
(b. 1812)
The West Indies in 1837. Being a Journal of a
Visit to Antigua, Montserrat, Dominica, St.
Lucia, Barbados and Jamaica. London: Hamilton,
Adams and Co., 1838. xi, 476, xcvp. (second
edition?) (Reprinted: New York, Barnes and
Noble, 1969.)

984. STURTZ, Johann Jacob (1800-77)
A Review, Financial, Statistical and Commercial
of the Empire of Brazil and its Resources. London: E. Wilson, 1837. viii, 151p.

985. SULLIVAN, Sir Edward Robert (1826-99)
Rambles and Scrambles in North and South America
[Venezuela, Guianas, etc.]. London: R. Bentley,
1852. viii, 424p.

986. (SUTCLIFFE, Thomas) (1790?-1849)
Sixteen Years in Chile and Peru [1822-39]. London: Fisher, Son and Co., 1841. xii, 563p.

987. SWETT, Charles
A Trip to British Honduras and to San Pedro,
Republic of Honduras. New Orleans: Price
Current Print Co., 1868. 135p.

T

988. TALBOYS, William P.
West India Pickles. Diary of a Cruise Through

the West Indies in the Yacht Josephine.   New
York: G. W. Carleton, 1876.   209p.

989.   TAYLOE, Edward Thornton
        Mexico, 1825-1828 [journal and correspondence].
        Chapel Hill: University of North Carolina Press,
        1959.   212p.   (edited by C. Harvey Gardiner.)

990.   TAYLOR, Bayard (1825-78)
        Eldorado, or Adventures in the Path of Empire
        [Mexico and Mexican War].   London: Henry Bohn
        1850.   2 volumes.   viii, 251, ii, 270p.   (Re-
        printed: Glorieta, N. M. , Rio Grande Press,
        1967; Palo Alto, Calif. , Lewis Osborne, 1968.)

991.   TAYLOR, Dr. Charles Edwin (b. 1843)
        The Island of the Sea [St. Thomas].   St. Thomas:
        Author, 1896.   120p.   (second edition?)

992.   TAYLOR, Dr. Charles Edwin
        Jumby Hall; A Story of the Danish West Indies.
        London: W. Dawson and Sons, 1890.   116p.

993.   TAYLOR, Dr. Charles Edwin
        Leaflets from the Danish West Indies [description
        of the three islands].   London: William Dawson,
        1888.   xv, 228p.   (Reprinted: Westport, Negro
        Universities Press, 1970.)

994.   T[A]YLOR, Edward Burnett[?] (b. 1832)
        Anahuac, or Mexico and the Mexicans, Ancient
        and Modern.   London: Publisher unknown, 1861.
        ?p. [see 1031.]

995.   TAYLOR, Rev. Fitch Waterman (1803-65)
        The Broad Pennant... [sketches of the Mexican
        War].   New York: Leavitt, Trow and Co. , 1848.
        415p.

996.   TAYLOR, Rev. Fitch Waterman
        The Flagship, or Voyage Around the World...
        [Brazil, Chile, Peru].   New York: D. Appleton,
        1840.   2 volumes.

997.   TAYLOR, John Glanville (1823-51)
        The United States and Cuba.   Eight Years of
        Change and Travel.   London: R. Bentley, 1851.
        xii, 328p.

998.   TAYLOR, John Metcalf (b. 1845)
       Maximilian and Carlotta.   A Story of Imperial-
       ism [history and description].   New York: G. P.
       Putnam, 1894. 209p.

999.   TAYLOR, William (1821-1902)
       Christian Adventures in South America.   London:
       Jackson, 1867. 557p.

1000. TAYLOR, William
       Our South American Cousins [Peru, Bolivia, Chile;
       1877-78]. New York: Nelson and Phillips, 1879
       (or 1878?). 318p.

1001. TEMPLE, Edmond
       Travels in Various Parts of Peru [and Bolivia;
       1825-26]. London: H. Colburn and R. Bentley,
       1830. 2 volumes. xvi, 431, viii, 504p. (Re-
       printed: New York, A. M. S. Press, 1971.)

1002. TEMPSKY, Gustav Ferdinand von
       Mitla: A Narrative of Incidents and Personal
       Adventures... [Guatemala, El Salvador, 1853-
       55]. London: Brown, Green, Longmans and
       Roberts, 1858. 436p. (edited by J. S. Bell.)

1003. TENNERY, Thomas D.
       Mexican War Diary, 1846-47. Norman: Uni-
       versity of Oklahoma Press, 1970. xl, 117p.
       (edited by D. E. Livingston-Little.)

1004. TERRELL, Alexander Watkins (1827-1912)
       From Texas to Mexico and the Court of Maxi-
       milian in 1865. Dallas: The Book Club of Texas,
       1933. xviii, 94p.

1005. TERRY, Adrian Russell (1808-64)
       Travels in the Equatorial Regions of South
       America in 1832 [Ecuador and Northern South
       America]. Hartford: Cooke and Co., 1834.
       290p.

1006. THOMAS, J. J.
       Froudacity: West Indian Fables by James
       Anthony Froude Explained. London: T. F. Un-
       win, 1889. 216p.

1007.   THOME, James A. and J. Horace Kimball (1813-38)
        Emancipation in the West Indies [six months tour
        in British West Indies, 1837]. New York: Ameri-
        can Anti-Slavery Society, 1838. 489p. (Reprinted:
        New York, Arno Press, 1969. 128p., abridged.)

1008.   THOMPSON, Lt. Col. George (1839-76)
        The War in Paraguay, with a Historical Sketch
        of the Country and its People.... London: Long-
        mans, Green and Co., 1869. x, 347p.

1009.   THOMPSON, George Alexander
        Handbook to the Pacific and California, Describing
        Eight Different Routes, by Sea; Central America,
        Mexico and the Territories of the United States.
        London: Simpkin and Marshall, 1849. 108p.

1010.   THOMPSON, George Alexander
        Narrative of an Official Visit to Guatemala from
        Mexico.... London: John Murray, 1829. xii,
        528p.

1011.   THOMPSON, James
        Letters on the Moral and Religious State of South
        America Written During a Residence of Nearly
        Seven Years in Buenos Aires, Chile, Peru and
        Colombia. London: James Nisbet, 1827. vi,
        296p.

1012.   THOMPSON, Waddy (1798-1868)
        Recollections of Mexico [1842-]. New York:
        Wiley, Putnam, 1846. x, 304p.; also London,
        1846.

1013.   THOMSON, Sir C. Nyville (1830-82)
        Voyage of the "Challenger" [Brazil, Argentina,
        Chile, etc.]. London: Macmillan, 1877. 2
        volumes.

1014.   (THOMSON, Capt. Joseph) (pseud: "An Officer of
        the Expedition")
        An Authentic Narrative... [British expedition to
        Montevideo and Buenos Aires]. London: The
        Author, 1808. viii, 216p.

1015.   TIERNAN, Mrs. Frances Christine Fisher (pseud:
        Christine Reid) (1846-1920)

The Land of the Sun; Vistas Mexicanas. New
York: D. Appleton and Co., 1894. 355p.

1016. TIERNAN, Mrs. Frances Christine Fisher
The Picture of Las Cruses. A Romance of
Mexico [fiction and description]. New York:
D. Appleton, 1896. 275p.

1017. TITFORD, William Jowit
Sketches Toward a Hortus Botanicus Americanus,
or Coloured Plates of New and Valuable Plants
in the West Indies and North and South America.
London: Sherwood, Neely and Jones, 1811. 190p.

1018. TOMES, Robert (1817-82)
Panama in 1855 [society; the railroad]. New York:
Harper and Brothers, 1855. 246p.

1019. TOWNSHEND, Frederick Trench
Wild Life in Florida, with a Visit to Cuba. London: Hurst and Blackett, 1875. 319p.

1020. ("A Traveler")
Notes and Reflections on Mexico, its Mines,
Policy ... By a Traveler. London: J. M. Rich-
ardson, 1827. ?p.

1021. TROLLOPE, Anthony (1815-82)
The West Indies and the Spanish Main [history
and description]. London: Chapman and Hall,
1859. iv, 395p. (Reprinted: New York, Barnes
and Noble, 1968.)

1022. TRUMAN, George; John Jackson; Thomas B. Long-
streth
Narrative of a Visit to the West Indies [Quakers
in the Lesser Antilles, 1840-1]. Philadelphia:
Merrihew and Thompson, 1844. 130p. (Reprinted:
Freeport, Books for Libraries, 1972.)

1023. TSCHUDI, Johann Jakob von (1818-89)
Travels in Peru During the Years 1838 to 1842, on
the Coast, in the Sierra, Across the Cordilleras
and the Andes, into the Primeval Forests. London: D. Bogue, 1847. xii, 606p. (translated
from German.)

1024.   (TUCKER, George)
        The Geography of America and the West Indies.
        London: Society for the Diffusion of Knowledge,
        1841. xii, 648p.

1025.   TUCKEY, James Kingston
        An Account of a Voyage... [Brazil, New South
        Wales, etc., 1802-4]. London: Longman, Hurst,
        Rees and Orme, Portsmouth, Mottley, 1805. xv,
        239p.

1026.   TUDOR, Henry
        Narrative of a Tour in North America; Comprising
        Mexico ... with an Excursion to the Island of
        Cuba [letters, 1831-32]. London: James Duncan,
        1834. 2 volumes. xix, 468, x, 548p.

1027.   TURNBULL, David
        The Jamaican Movement for Promoting the En-
        forcement of the Slave Trade Treaties and the
        Suppression of the Slave Trade... [history and
        description]. London: Longman? 1850. 430p.
        (Reprinted: Westport, Negro Universities Press,
        1971.)

1028.   TURNBULL, David
        Travels in the West.   Cuba; with Notices of
        Porto Rico and the Slave Trade.   London: Long-
        man, Orme, Brown, Green and Longmans, 1840.
        xvi, 574p. (Reprinted: Westport, Negro Univer-
        sities Press, 1971.)

1029.   TURNER, Thomas A.
        Argentina and the Argentines [1885-90]. New York:
        Charles Scribner's Sons, 1892. xvi, 370p.; also
        London, 1892.

1030.   TWEEDIE, Ethel Brilliano (Harley) (d. 1940)
        Mexico as I Saw It [end of century]. London:
        Hurst and Blackett, 1901. xii, 472p.

1031.   TYLOR, Sir Edward Bennett (1832-1917)
        Anahuac, or Mexico and the Mexicans, Ancient
        and Modern. London: Longman, Green, Long-
        mans and Roberts, 1861. xvii, 344p. (Reprinted:
        New York, Bergman, 1970.)

1032.   (TYNG, C. D.) ?
        The Stranger in the Tropics [Cuba, Puerto Rico,
        St. Thomas]. New York: American News Co.,
        1868. 194p.

                            U

1033.   UDELL, John (b. 1795)
        Incidents of Travel to California, Across the Great
        Plains, with the Return Trips Through Central
        America and Jamaica. Jefferson, Ohio: Sentinel
        Office, 1856. 302p.

1034.   UHLE, Max Friedrich (b. 1856)
        Pachacamac. Report of the William Pepper ...
        Peruvian Expedition of 1896. Philadelphia: Uni-
        versity of Pennsylvania, 1903. xi, 103p.

1035.   UNDERHILL, Edward Bean (1813-1901)
        The Tragedy of Morant Bay. A Narrative of
        the Disturbances in the Island of Jamaica in 1865.
        London: Alexander and Sapheard, 1895. xix,
        219p.

1036.   UNDERHILL, Edward Bean
        The West Indies; Their Social and Religious Con-
        dition. London: Colchester, 1862. x, 493p.
        (Reprinted: Westport, Negro Universities Press,
        1971.)

                            V

1037.   VASTEY, Pompeé Valentin, Baron de
        An Essay on the Causes of the Revolution and
        Civil Wars of Hayti.... Exater: Western
        Luminary Office, 1823. 249p. (Reprinted:
        Westport, Negro Universities Press, 1971.)

1038.   VENESS, Rev. William Thomas
        El Dorado, or British Guiana as a Field for
        Colonization [missionary resident for ten years].
        London: Cassell, 1866. 198p.

1039.   VENESS, Rev. William Thomas
        Ten Years of Mission Life in British Guiana.

London: Society for Promoting Christian Knowl-
edge, 1875. 136p.

1040. VERNON, B. J.
Early Recollections of Jamaica [before 1812].
London: Whittaker and Co., 1848. 200p.

1041. VIDAL, Emeric Essex
Picturesque Illustrations of Buenos Aires and
Montevideo [colored illustrations]. London: R.
Ackerman, 1820. xxviii, 115p.

1042. VIGNE, Godfrey Thomas (1801-63)
Travels in Mexico, South America, etc....
London: Allen and Co., 1863. 2 volumes. iv,
374, 317p.

1043. VILLAFRANCA, Richard
Costa Rica, the Gem of the American Republics.
New York: Sackett and Whilhelms, 1895. 139p.

1044. VINCENT, Frank (1848-1916)
Around and About South America... [1885-87].
New York: D. Appleton and Co., 1890. xxiv,
473p.

1045. VINCENT, Frank
In and Out of Central America [and Asia]. New
York: D. Appleton and Co., 1890. viii, 246p.

1046. VINCENT, Mrs. Howard (Ethel Gwendoline Moffant
Vincent) (b. 1861)
China to Peru Over the Andes. A Journey
Through South America [Peru, Chile, Argentina,
Brazil, Venezuela, Panama]. London: Sampson
Low, Marston and Co., 1894. x, 333p.

1047. VOWELL, Richard Longeville
Campaigns and Cruises... [Venezuela, Colombia,
Chile, etc.]. London: Longman, 1831. 3
volumes.

W

1048. WADDELL, Hope Masterton
Twenty-nine Years in the West Indies and Central

Africa [as missionary, 1829-58]. London: T.
Nelson, 1863. xiv, 681p. (Reprinted: London,
Frank Cass, 1970.)

1049.   (WALKER, Alexander)
        Colombia: Being a Geographical, Statistical,
        Agricultural, Commercial and Political Account
        of that Country. London: Baldwin, Cradock and
        Joy, 1822. 2 volumes.

1050.   WALKER, General William (1824-60)
        The War in Nicaragua. Mobile: S. H. Goetzel,
        1860. 431p. (Reprinted: Detroit, Blaire
        Ethridge, 1971.)

1051.   WALLACE, Alfred Russel (1823-1913) (sometimes
        listed under Richard Spruce)
        A Narrative of Travels on the Amazon and Río
        Negro, with an Account of the Native Tribes
        [during four years]. London: Reeve and Co.,
        1852-3. 2 volumes. lii, 518, viii, 541p. (many
        editions, some abridged.) (Reprinted: New York,
        Haskell House, 1969; Westport, Greenwood, 1969;
        New York, Dover, 1972.)

1052.   WALLACE, Susan Arnold Elston (pseud: "Mrs. Lew
        Wallace") (1830-1907)
        The Land of the Pueblos [southwest United States
        and Mexico]. New York: J. B. Alden, 1888.
        285p.

1053.   WALLBRIDGE, Edwin Angel (editor)
        The Demerara Martyr. Memoir of the Rev. John
        Smith, Missionary to Demerara, 1848 [diary;
        Guiana and Janaica; slaves; missions]. London:
        Publisher unknown, 1848. 274p. (Reprinted:
        London, Frank Cass, 1972? 106p.)

1054.   WALLER, John Augustine
        A Voyage to the West Indies [Barbados and Lee-
        ward islands]. London: Sir R. Phillips, 1820.
        106p.

1055.   WALPOLE, Frederick (1822-76)
        Four Years in the Pacific [and South America,
        1844-48]. London: R. Bentley, 1849. 2 volumes.
        xiii, 432, ix, 415p.

1056.   WALSH, Rev. Robert (1772-1852)
        Notices of Brazil in 1828 and 1829 [chiefly Rio
        de Janeiro]. London: F. Westley and A. H.
        Davis, 1830. 2 volumes. xv, 528, xii, 541p.

1057.   WALTON, William (1784-1857)
        An Exposé on the Dissensions of Spanish America
        [and suggested British intervention]. London:
        The Author, 1814. viii, 480p.

1058.   WALTON, William
        Historical and Descriptive Account of the Peruvian
        Sheep, Called Carneros de la Tierra [sheep
        raising etc.]. London: J. Harding, 1811. 183p.

1059.   WALTON, William
        Present State of the Spanish Colonies [and His-
        paniola]. London: Longman, Rees, Orme and
        Brown, 1810. 2 volumes. xiv, 384, vii, 386p.

1060.   WARD, Sir Henry George
        Mexico in 1827 [and 1825, 1826]. London: H.
        Colburn, 1828. 2 volumes. (second enlarged
        edition, 1829.)

1061.   WARNER, Charles Dudley (1829-1900)
        On Horseback... [Mexico, California, part of
        Eastern United States]. Boston: Houghton,
        Mifflin, 1888. 331p.

1062.   WARREN, John Esaias
        Pará, Scenes and Adventures on the Banks of the
        Amazon. New York: G. P. Putnam, 1851. iv,
        271p.

1063.   WARREN, Thomas Robinson (1828-1915)
        Dust and Foam; or, Three Oceans and Two Con-
        tinents... [Mexico, West Indies, South America].
        London: Sampson Low, 1840. xiii, 397p.

1064.   WASHBURN, Charles Ames (1822-89)
        The History of Paraguay with Notes of Personal
        Observations.... Boston: Lee, Shepard and
        Dillingham, 1871. xii, 571, xvip. (Reprinted:
        New York, A. M. S. Press, 1969.)

1065.   WATERTON, Charles (1782-1865)
        Wanderings in South America, the North-West of
        the United States and the Antilles in the Years
        1812, 1816, 1820 and 1824 [especially Brazil, the
        Guianas, etc.]. London: J. Mawman, 1825. vii,
        326p. (Reprinted: Upper Saddle River, N.J.,
        Gregg Press, 1968.)

1066.   WEATHERHEAD, W. Davidson
        Account of the Expedition Against the Isthmus of
        Darien [under Gregor McGregor]. London: Long-
        man, Hurst, Rees, Orme and Brown, 1821. 134p.

1067.   WEBBER, Vivian Arthur
        Journal of a Voyage Around Cape Horn [Chile].
        Swansea: W.W. Bruster, 1859. vii, 163p.

1068.   WEBSTER, William Henry Bayley (sometimes listed
        under Capt. Henry Foster, 1796-1831)
        Narrative of a Voyage to the South Atlantic Ocean
        [journal of a surgeon; east coast of South America,
        1828-30]. London: William Bentley, 1834. 2
        volumes. xi, 399, viii, 398p.

1069.   WEDDELL, James (1787-1834)
        Voyage Towards the South Pole, 1822-1824, and a
        Visit to Tierra de Fuego, with a Particular Ac-
        count of the Inhabitants.... London: Longman,
        Hurst, Rees, Orme, Brown and Green, 1825. iv,
        276p. (Reprinted: Annapolis, U.S. Naval Acad-
        emy, 1971.)

1070.   WELBY-Gregory, Victoria Alexandrina Maria Louisa
        Stuart-Wortley (1837-1912)
        A Young Traveller's Journal of a Tour in North
        and South America During the Year 1850. London:
        T. Bosworth, 1852. xii, 260p.

1071.   WELLES, C.M.
        Three Years' Wanderings of a Connecticut Yankee
        in South America, Africa, Australia and California.
        New York: American Subscription Publishing House,
        1859. 358p.

1072.   WELLS, David Ames (1825-98)
        A Study of Mexico. New York: D. Appleton,
        1887. 261p. (Reprinted: Clifton, N.J., A.M.
        Kelley, 1971.)

1073. WELLS, James William
       Exploring and Traveling 3000 Miles Through Brazil
       [from Rio de Janeiro to Maranhão]. Philadelphia:
       J. B. Lippincott, 1886. 2 volumes. xx, 411, xii,
       386p.; also London, 1886.

1074. WELLS, James William
       The Voyce of Urbano; or, the Indian Slaves of the
       Amazon. London: W. H. Allen and Co., 1889.
       viii, 394p. (second edition?)

1075. WELLS, W.
       Notes of a Journey from the River St. Francisco
       to the River Tocantins and to the City of Maranhão.
       Philadelphia: Publisher unknown, 1876. ?p.

1076. WELLS, William Vincent (1826-76)
       Explorations and Adventures in Honduras [and
       Central America]. New York: Harper and
       Brothers, 1857. 588p.

1077. WELLS, William Vincent
       Walker's Expedition to Nicaragua [history, biog-
       raphy, description of people, places]. New York:
       Stringer and Townsend, 1856. 316p.

1078. (WENTWORTH, Trelaway)
       The West India Sketch Book [in late 1820s]. Lon-
       don: Whittaker and Co., 1834. 2 volumes. x,
       324, vi, 391p.

1079. WEATHERELL, James (1822?-1858)
       Brazil, Stray Notes from Bahia [letters covering
       15 years]. Liverpool: Binkenhead, 1860. viii,
       153p.

1080. WHEAT, Marvin
       Travels in the Western Slopes of the Mexican
       Cordillera [51 letters]. San Francisco: Whitton,
       Towne and Co., 1857. 438p.

1081. WHEELER, Maj. Gen. Joseph (1836-1906)
       The Santiago Campaign, 1898 [Cuba]. Philadelphia:
       Drexel Biddle, 1898. xviii, 369p. (Reprinted:
       Port Washington, Kennikat Press, 1971.)

1082.   WHITE, Ernest William
         Cameos from the Silver-Land, or the Experiences
         of a Young Naturalist in the Argentine Republic.
         London: J. Van Voorst, 1881-2. 2 volumes.
         xviii, 436, xvi, 527p.

1083.   WHITE, Capt. T. Melville
         Britons, Robbed, Tortured and Murdered in Peru
         [1860-1? under Castilla]. London: Robert Hard-
         wicke, 1862. xx, 148p.

1084.   WHITE, Trumbull (b. 1868)
         Our New Possessions [descriptions of Cuba,
         Puerto Rico, Philippines, Hawaii]. Chicago:
         Henry Publishing Co., 1898. 676p.

1085.   WHITE, Trumbull
         United States in War with Spain and the History
         of Cuba [description of Cuba]. Chicago: Inter-
         national Publishing Co., 1898. 566p.

1086.   WHITELOCKE, John
         The Proceedings of a General Court Martial...
         [of British Commander in La Plata, 1806-7].
         London: Longman, Hurst, Rees and Orme, 1808.
         2 volumes. xxxix, 830p.

1087.   WHITTLE, W.
         Journal of a Voyage to the River Plate [and a
         residence in Uruguay]. Manchester: Bradshaw
         and Blacklock, 1846. 102p.

1088.   WHYMPER, Edward (1840-1911)
         Travels Amongst the Great Andes of the Equator
         [1879-]. London: John Murray, 1891. 2
         volumes. (including Supplementary Appendix.)
         xxiv, 456, xvii, 147p.

1089.   WICHKAM, Sir Henry Alexander (1846-1928)
         Rough Notes of a Journey Through the Wilderness
         from Trinidad to Pará [and Central America,
         1869-]. London: W. H. J. Carter, 1872. viii,
         301p.

1090.   WIED-Neuwied, Maximilian Alexander Phillipp,
         Prinz von (1782-1867)
             Travels in Brazil [1815-1817]. London: R. Phillips,
             1820. Part I, iv, 112p. (translated from German.)

1091.   WIENER, Charles (1851-1913)
        Chile and the Chileans. Paris: L. Cerf, 1888.
        381p. (3rd edition)

1092.   WILBERFORCE, Edward (b. 1834)
        Brazil Viewed Through a Naval Glass.... London:
        Longman, Brown, Green and Longmans, 1856.
        x, 236p.

1093.   WILBERFORCE, William (1759-1833) and Z.
        Macaulay
        Slavery in the West Indies [description]. London:
        No publisher, 1823. 2 articles bound together.
        56, 92p. (Reprinted: Westport, Negro Univer-
        sities Press, 1969.)

1094.   WILCOCKE, Samuel Hull
        History of the Viceroyalty of Buenos Aires
        [description: commerce, population, government,
        etc.]. London: Sherwood, Neely and Jones,
        1807. 576p.

1095.   WILCOX, Gen. Cadmus Marcellus (1826-90)
        History of the Mexican War [and description].
        Washington: Church News Publishing Co., 1892.
        x, 711p.

1096.   WILEMAN, J. P.
        Brazilian Exchange; the Study of an inconvertable
        Currency [the economy]. Buenos Aires: Gelli
        Brothers, 1896. xvi, 267p. (Reprinted: West-
        port, Greenwood, 1969?)

1097.   WILKES, Charles (1798-1877)
        Narratives of the United States Exploring Expedi-
        tion During the Years 1838 ... 1842 [South
        America in volume one]. Philadelphia: Lea and
        Blanchard, 1844. 5 volumes. Vol. 1, lxvi,
        455p.

1098.   WILKINS, James Hepburn
        A Glimpse of Old Mexico; Being the Observations
        and Reflections of a Tenderfoot Editor [mining in
        Durango]. San Rafael, California: The Author,
        1901. 115p.

1099.   WILLIAMS, Alfred Mason
        Under the Trade Winds [West Indies].   Providence:
        Preston and Rounds, 1889.   x, 162p.

1100.   WILLIAMS, Cynric R.
        A Tour Through the Island of Jamaica from the
        Western to the Eastern end in the Year 1823
        [during about three months].   London: Hunt and
        Clarke, 1826.   xviii, 352p.

1101.   WILLIAMS, Rose Carnegie
        A Year in the Andes, or a Lady's Adventures in
        Bogotá.   London: London Literary Society, 1881.
        270p.

1102.   WILLIAMS, William Frith
        An Historical and Statistical Account of the Ba-
        hamas [from discovery].   London: T. C. Newby,
        1848.   346p.

1103.   WILLIAMSON, John Gustavus Adolphus
        Caracas Diary, 1834-40.   Baton Rouge: Camellia
        Publishing Co., 1954.   xxiv, 444p.

1104.   WILLIS, Nathaniel Parker (1806-67)
        A Health Trip to the Tropics [letters from the
        West Indies and the United States].   New York:
        Charles Scribners, 1853.   xiii, 421, +23p.

1105.   WILSON, James (1799-1827)
        A Brief Memoir ... Written Chiefly During a
        Residence in Guatemala.   London: A. Panton,
        1829.   iv, 165p.

1106.   WILSON, Robert Anderson (1812-72)
        Mexico and its Religion, with Incidents of Travel
        in that Country During Parts of the Years 1851,
        1852, 1853, 1854.   New York: Harper and
        Brothers, 1855.   406p.

1107.   WILSON, Robert Anderson
        Mexico, Including California and Central America
        [during seven years of travel].   New York:
        Harper and Brothers, 1855.   436p.

1108.   WILSON, Robert Anderson
        Mexico.   Its Peasants and its Priests [1851-55].

New York: Harper and Brothers, 1856.   418p.
("new edition")

1109.   WILSON, Thomas
        Transatlantic Sketches; or Travelling Reminiscences
        of the West Indies and the United States.   Mont-
        real: J. Lovell, 1860.   xi, 179p.

1110.   WINEFRED, Landy (pseud. for Howard of Gloscop)
        Journal of a Tour in the United States, Canada
        and Mexico [seven chapters on Mexico].   London:
        Publisher unknown, 1897.   355p.

1111.   WINN, T. S.
        Emancipation: or, Practical Advice to British
        Slave-Holders.   With Suggestions for the General
        Improvement of West India Affairs.   London: W.
        Phillips, 1824.   111p.   (Reprinted: Westport,
        Negro Universities Press, 1971.)

1112.   WINTHROP, Theodore (1826-61)
        The Canoe and the Saddle; Adventures Among the
        Northern Rivers and Forests; and the Isthmiana
        [Panama, etc.].   Boston: Ticknor and Fields,
        1863.   375p.

1113.   WISE, Lt. Henry Augustus (1819-69?)
        Los Gringos, or, an Inside View of Mexico and
        California [also Chile, Peru and Brazil].   New
        York: Baker and Scribner, 1849.   xvi, 453p.; a
        shorter London edition, 1849.

1114.   WISLIZENUS, Frederick Adolphus (1810-89)
        Memoir of a Tour to Northern Mexico, Connected
        with Col. Doniphan's Expedition in 1846 and 1847
        [along Rio Grande, etc.].   Washington: Tippin
        and Streeper, 1848.   141p.   (Reprinted: Glorieta,
        N. M., Rio Grande Press, 1969.)

1115.   WOOD, Walter E.
        Venezuela, or Two Years on the Spanish Main.
        London: Simpkin, Marshall, Hamilton, and Kent,
        1896.   xxxii, 196p.

1116.   WOODCOCK, Henry Iles
        A History of Tobago [and description].   Ayr:
        Smith and Grant, 1867.   195p.   (Reprinted: Lon-
        don, Frank Cass, 1971.)

1117. WOODCOCK, Henry Iles
       The Laws and Constitutions of the British Colonies
       in the West Indies having Legislative Assemblies.
       London: R. and W. Swale, 1828. xii, 304p.

1118. WORTLEY, Lady Ammeline Charlotte Elizabeth
       (Manners) Stuart (1806-55)
       Travels in the United States During 1849 and 1850
       [with about 100 pages on Mexico]. New York:
       Harper and Brothers, 1851. 463p.

1119. (WORTLEY, Victoria Stuart) (pseud. for Lady Am-
       meline Charlotte Elizabeth (Manners) Stuart)
       Young Traveller's Tour in North and South America
       During the Year 1850 [for children and adults].
       London: T. Bosworth, 1852. xii, 260p.

1120. WRAY, John
       The Life and Labours of... [diaries and writings
       of a pioneer missionary in British Guiana]. Lon-
       don: Publisher unknown, 1892. v, 376p. (edited
       by Thomas Rain.)

1121. Wright, Marie Robinson (1866-1914)
       The New Brazil... [2000 miles journey during two
       years]. Philadelphia: George Berrie, 1901.
       450p.; also London, 1901.

1122. Wright, Marie Robinson
       Picturesque Mexico. Philadelphia: J.B. Lippin-
       cott, 1897. 445p.

1123. WURDEMANN, Dr. John George F. (1810-49)
       Notes on Cuba... [a physician's experiences].
       Boston: J. Munro and Co., 1844. x, 359p.
       (Reprinted: New York, Arno Press, 1971.)

                              Y

1124. YOUNG, Philip
       History of Mexico... [and description]. New York:
       J.S. Redfield, 1847. 564p.; also Cincinnati, 1847.

1125. YOUNG, Thomas
       Narrative of a Residence on the Mosquito Shore

During the Years 1839, 1840 and 1841.   London:
Smith, Elder and Co. , 1842.   iv, 172p.   (Reprinted: New York, Kraus, 1971.)

1126.   YOUNG, Sir William (1749-1815)
The West Indies Common-Place Book... [the
sugar colonies, compiled from documents, etc.].
London: Richard Phillips, 1807.   xxi, 256p.

Z

1127.   ZAREMBA, Charles W.
The Merchants' and Tourists' Guide to Mexico.
Chicago: Althrop Publishing House, 1883.   182p.

1128. Alta California [Mexican War; California and North
Mexico]. Philadelphia: H. Packer and Co.,
1847. 331p.

1129. Argentine Republic; a Handbook. Washington:
Bureau of American Republics, 1892. vi, 455p.
(Reprinted: Washington, 1894; revised.)

1130. Bolivia; a Handbook. Washington: Bureau of American Republics, 1893. vi, 413p.

1131. Brazil, the Amazon and the Coast [description].
New York: Publisher unknown, 1879. ?p.

1132. Brazil, A Handbook. Washington: Bureau of
American Republics, 1891. 336p.

1133. Colombia. Boston: The Modern Traveler, 1830.
336p.

1134. Colombia: a Handbook. Washington: Bureau of
American Republics, 1892. 138p.

1135. Commercial Directory of the American Republics
[Mexico, Nicaragua, Paraguay, Peru, Salvador,
Santo Domingo, United States, Uruguay, Vene-
zuela, and the West Indies]. Washington:
Bureau of American Republics, 1893. 458p.
(Reprinted: 2 volumes, 1897-8. 1589p.; re-
vised.)

1136. Commercial Directory of Mexico. Washington:
Bureau of American Republics, 1891. iii, 122p.

1137. Commercial Information Concerning the American
Republics and Colonies. Washington: Bureau of
American Republics, 1892. 286p.

1138. Commercial Mission to South America. Washington:
Bureau of American Republics, 1899. 178p.

1139. A Complete Historical, Chronological and Geographical
       American Atlas... [a guide to North and South
       America and the West Indies to 1822]. Phila-
       delphia: Carey and Lea, 1822. 118p.

1140. A Condensed Report of the Transactions of the Com-
       mission and of the Surveys and Explorations of
       its Engineers in Central America and South
       America, 1891-1898. Washington: Inter Conti-
       nental Railway Commission, 1895-98. 3 volumes
       in 4.

1141. Costa Rica: a Handbook. Washington: Bureau of
       American Republics, 1892. iv, 146p.

1142. A Diary of the Wreck of His Majesty's Ship Chal-
       lenger, on the Western Coast of South America,
       in May 1835 [seven weeks on the south coast of
       Chile]. London: Longman, Reese, Orme, Brown,
       Green and Longman, 1836. 160p. [see 862.]

1143. The Earth Delineated with Pen and Pencil [Cuba,
       etc.]. London: Publisher unknown, date?
       413p.

1144. Ecuador; a Handbook. Washington: Bureau of Ameri-
       can Republics, 1894. v, 177p. (Reprinted:
       Washington, 1896; revised.)

1145. Foreign Commerce of the American Republics and
       Colonies. Washington: Bureau of American
       Republics, 1892. 171p. (Reprinted: Washing-
       ton, 1897; revised.)

1146. Guatemala: a Handbook. Washington: Bureau of
       American Republics, 1892. 192p. (Reprinted:
       Washington, 1897; revised.)

1147. Haiti; a Handbook. Washington: Bureau of American
       Republics, 1893. 240p.

1148. Handbook of the American Republics. Washington:
       Bureau of American Republics, 1891. 486p.
       (Reprinted: Washington, 1893; revised.)

1149. Harper's Pictorial History of the War with Spain.
       New York: Harper, 1899. 2 volumes. vii, 507p.

1150.   Honduras: a Handbook. Washington: Bureau of
        American Republics, 1892. vi, 186p. (Reprinted:
        Washington, 1894, 1895; revised.)

1151.   How the Latin American Markets may be Reached by
        the Manufacturers of the United States [descrip-
        tions]. Washington: Bureau of American Re-
        publics, 1893. ix, 505p.

1152.   Laws of the American Republics Relating to Immi-
        gration and the Sale of Land. Washington:
        Bureau of American Republics, 1893. iv, 199p.

1153.   Letters from the Virgin Islands, Illustrating Life
        and Manners in the West Indies. London: J.
        Van Voorst, 1843. x, 286p.

1154.   Mexico: The Country, History and People. London:
        Religious Tract Society, 1863. viii, 340p.

1155.   Mexico, a Geographical Sketch. Washington: Bureau
        of American Republics, 1900. 385p.

1156.   Mexico in 1842. New York: Publisher unknown,
        1842. 256p.

1157.   Mines and Mining Laws of Latin America. Washing-
        ton: Bureau of American Republics, 1892. 348p.

1158.   Nicaragua; a Handbook. Washington: Bureau of
        American Republics, 1890. 183p. (Reprinted:
        Washington, 1892; revised.)

1159.   Paraguay; a Handbook. Washington: Bureau of
        American Republics, 1895. vi, 146p.

1160.   Peru: a Handbook. Washington: Bureau of Ameri-
        can Republics, 1895. iii, 145p.

1161.   Popular Description, Geographical, Historical, and
        Topographical of Mexico and Guatemala. Boston:
        Wells and Lilly, 1830. 2 volumes; also Phila-
        delphia, 1830.

1162.   The Present State of Colombia, Containing an Account
        of the Principle Events of its Revolutionary War.
        London: J. Murray, 1827. iv, 336p.

1163.   Recollections of Services [in Venezuela and Colombia
        during three years of war]. London: Hunt and
        Clarke, 1828. 2 volumes. 263, 277p.

1164.   Report of the Royal Commission to Inquire into the
        Condition and Affairs of the Island of Dominica
        and Correspondence Relating Thereto. London:
        Publisher unknown, 1894. 204p.

1165.   Reports of Explorations and Survey for the Location
        of a Ship-Canal between the Atlantic and Pacific
        Oceans through Nicaragua, 1872-73. Washing-
        ton: Government Printing Office, 1874. 143p.
        and maps.

1166.   The Republic of Guatemala, 1897. Washington:
        Bureau of American Republics, 1897. vi, 119p.

1167.   The Republic of Uruguay, South America... [pre-
        pared by Consulate]. London: E. Stanford,
        1883. xii, 168p.

1168.   Salvador: a Handbook. Washington: Bureau of
        American Republics, 1895. vi, 169p.

1169.   Santo Domingo Commission. Report of the Com-
        mission of Inquiry to Santo Domingo. Washing-
        ton: Government Printing Office, 1871. 297p.

1170.   Santo Domingo; a Handbook. Washington: Bureau
        of American Republics, 1895. vi, 202p.

1171.   A Sketch of the Customs and Society of Mexico in a
        Series of Familiar Letters; and a Journal of
        Travels in the Interior during the Years 1824,
        1825, 1826. London: Longman and Co., 1828.
        242p.

1172.   A Sketch of the Route to California and Japan via
        the Isthmus of Panama; A Useful and Amusing
        Book to Every Traveller. San Francisco: A.
        Roman and Co., 1867. 104p.

1173.   The Spanish American War. The Events of the
        War Described by an Eye-Witness. Chicago:
        H. B. Stone and Co., 1899. 228p.

1174. Summer Leisure. New York: The Tribune Association, 1890. 100p.

1175. Tariffs of the American Republics. Washington:
       Bureau of American Republics, 1893. 3 volumes.

1176. The Tehuantepec Railway. Its Location, Features
       and Advantages under the La Sere Grant of 1869
       [Mexico]. New York: D. Appleton and Co.,
       1869. xxii, 88p., map case.

1177. United States-Venezuela Boundary Commission.
       Report and Accompanying Papers. Washington:
       Government Printing Office, 1897. 3 volumes.

1178. Uruguay; A Handbook. Washington: Bureau of
       American Republics, 1893. vi, 347p.

1179. Venezuela; A Handbook. Washington: Bureau of
       American Republics, 1892. iii, 199p. (Reprinted: Washington, 1899; revised in 2 volumes.)

1180. The War and its Warriors [armies and leaders; anecdotes and sketches]. Philadelphia: Hogan and
       Thompson, 1848. 319p.

1181. West Indian Slavery: Selected Pamphlets. London:
       Allerton and Henderson, 1816-17. 683p. (Reprinted: Westport, Greenwood Press, 1971.)

1182. West Indies Sketch Book. London: Publisher unknown, 1835. 2 volumes.

GEOGRAPHICAL INDEX

prepared by

Gilberto V. Fort
Instructional Resources, Miami Dade Junior College

Note: The first number indicates the numbered item in the
Bibliography. The numbers in parentheses indicate the date
of the event described or the date of the publication of the
account.

AMERICAN REPUBLICS

1137.	(1892)
1145.	(1892, 1897)
1148.	(1891, 1893)
1152.	(1893)
1175.	(1893)

ANDES

141.	(1857)
195.	(1881-82)
202.	(1867)
627.	(1877)
637.	(1849-52)
653.	(1887)
945.	(1849-64)

ANTIGUA

376.	(1844)
753.	(1894-99)
983.	(1838)

ANTILLES

433.	(1881)
744.	(1888)

ARGENTINA

8.	(1893)
18.	(1825-26)
21.	(1817-20)
27.	(1891)
41.	(1887)
72.	(1828)
97.	(1854-55)
119.	(1817-18)
121.	(1828)
123.	(1878)
177.	(1819-21)

220.	(1876-77)
225.	(1880-)
248.	(1845)
249.	(1825)
256.	(1888-1900)
268.	(1871-)
270.	(1896)
279.	(1857)
287.	(1852, 1893-94)
293.	(1819)
294.	(1805)
303.	(1854)
313.	(1887-)
316.	(1876)
341.	(1887)
354.	(1889)
364.	(1877)
365.	(1829)
370.	(1872)
374.	(1899)
389.	(1826)
407.	(1840)
412.	(1808)
415.	(1854)
416.	(1869)
417.	(1853)
420.	(1893)
422.	(1806-07)
448.	(1853)
449.	(1868)
450.	(1870-76)
451.	(1829)
485.	(1827)
486.	(1825-26)
490.	(1806)
496.	(1821)
501.	(1863)
503.	(1887)
516.	(1892)
527.	(1862-63)
528.	(1860)
549.	(1841-44)
552.	(1868)
564.	(1869)
568.	(1892)
577.	(1846)

BRAZIL

146.   (1854)
167.   (1898)
173.   (1830s and 1840s)
177.   (1819-21)
227.   (1817-)
234.   (1860)
235.   (1820s)
236.   (1817-25)
240.   (1817-19)
248.   (1845)
252.   (1829)
256.   (1888-1900)
261.   (1845)
265.   (1864)
268.   (1871-)
270.   (1896)
281.   (1881)
293.   (1819)
305.   (1817)
316.   (1876)
346.   (1849)
374.   (1899)
407.   (1840)
415.   (1854)
417.   (1853)
424.   (1849-52)
434.   (1822)
450.   (1870-76)
451.   (1829)
456.   (1820-22)
486.   (1825-26)
495.   (1891)
496.   (1824)
500.   (1876)
523.   (1866)
554.   (1816)
589.   (1883)
647.   (1879-82)
658.   (1821-27)
662.   (1825)
677.   (1853-)
679.   (1819-35)
697.   (1897)
738.   (1874)
771.   (1855-59)
793.   (1812-14)
807.   (1823-24)

832.   (1862-63)
862.   (1835)
867.   (1841-63)
888.   (1820-21)
917.   (1817)
929.   (1849-52)
933.   (1899)
968.   (1867-69)
971.   (1805-25)
979.   (1849)
986.   (1832-39)
996.   (1840)
1000. (1877-78)
1013. (1877)
1046. (1894)
1047. (1831)
1091. (1888)
1113. (1849)

COLOMBIA

14.   (1814-26)
19.   (1860)
33.   (1822-23)
49.   (1893)
76.   (1843)
101. (late 19th century)
109. (1860)
179. (1894)
195. (1881-82)
232. (1823-24)
250. (1825)
312. (1850)
325. (1822 and 1823)
326. (1807)
349. (1836)
457. (1824)
464. (1827)
470. (1823)
508. (1852-53)
537. (1890)
626. (1838)
686. (1891)
691. (1822-23)
693. (1838)
750. (1783-1826)

714. (1854)
715. (1855)
718. (1899)
719. (1898)
725. (1898)
732. (1870)
736. (1845)
748. (1897)
749. (1874)
752. (1899)
755. (1898)
776. (1899)
779. (1856)
782. (1857)
796. (1899)
808. (1898)
809. (1898)
810. (1896)
817. (1897)
835. (1889)
856. (1852)
864. (1896)
873. (1872)
921. (1898)
934. (1885)
958. (1881)
997. (1851)
1019. (1875)
1026. (1831-32)
1028. (1840)
1032. (1868)
1081. (1898)
1084. (1898)
1085. (1898)
1123. (1844)
1143. (?)
1149. (1899)
1173. (1899)

CURAÇAO

849. (1892)

DANISH WEST INDIES

992. (1890)
993. (1888)

DEMERARA

149. (1824)
671. (1824)
1053. (1848)

DOMINICA

983. (1838)
1164. (1894)

DUTCH GUIANA

764. (1876)
870. (1805-7)

EAST COAST OF
SOUTH AMERICA

315. (1893)
1068. (1828-30)

ECUADOR

76. (1843)
109. (1860)
312. (1850)
479. (1867)
754. (1867-)
778. (1852)
924. (1877?)
953. (1850)
1005. (1834)
1088. (1879-)
1144. (1894, 1896)

HONDURAS

24.	(1820-23)
36.	(1850)
208.	(1890)
532.	(1856)
605.	(1866)
612.	(1887)
699.	(1897)
721.	(1871)
887.	(1857)
937.	(1884)
946.	(1870)
947.	(1857)
949.	(1855)
987.	(1868)
1076.	(1857)
1150.	(1892, 1894 and 1895)

JAMAICA

34.	(1890)
88.	(1825)
90.	(1850)
102.	(1853)
130.	(1827-28)
151.	(1854)
157.	(1823-46)
195.	(1881-82)
196.	(1846)
203.	(1803)
274.	(1801-15)
282.	(1803)
286.	(1819)
367.	(1890)
371.	(1865)
387.	(1831-32)
399.	(late 19th century)
410.	(1872)
431.	(1847)
432.	(1851)
460.	(1809)
476.	(1866)
532.	(1856)
576.	(1850)

604.	(1815-17)
639.	(1835)
688.	(1839)
692.	(1899)
740.	(1801-05)
781.	(1843)
813.	(1873)
823.	(1807)
863.	(1823)
907.	(1835)
957.	(1898)
966.	(1837)
974.	(1808)
975.	(1823)
983.	(1838)
1027.	(1850)
1033.	(1856)
1035.	(1865)
1040.	(before 1812)
1053.	(1848)
1100.	(1823)

LATIN AMERICA (GENERAL)

40.	(1872)
84.	(1844)
105.	(1827)
135.	(1868)
171.	(19th century)
277.	(1888)
355.	(1827)
386.	(1893)
401.	(1860-63)
428.	(1852)
520.	(1814)
521.	(1799-1804)
593.	(1852)
803.	(1874-)
1135.	(1893)
1151.	(1893)
1157.	(1892)

251.	(1825)	442.	(1886)
253.	(1892)	452.	(1886)
254.	(1883)	453.	(1888)
255.	(1883)	456.	(1820-22)
258.	(1857)	459.	(1864-65)
264.	(1848-49)	462.	(1898)
267.	(1889)	465.	(1881)
280.	(1883)	466.	(1883)
299.	(1831)	467.	(1882)
300.	(1889)	471.	(1825-28)
306.	(1889-90)	475.	(1863)
319.	(1858)	480.	(1875)
320.	(1847)	493.	(1847)
324.	(1874-87)	497.	(1892)
330.	(1891)	499.	(1849-50)
331.	(1860)	504.	(1872)
342.	(1836)	507.	(1895)
345.	(1867)	510.	(1844)
348.	(1857)	514.	(1892)
350.	(1846-48)	519.	(1811)
353.	(1868-70)	525.	(1825)
362.	(1876)	532.	(1856)
363.	(1890)	538.	(1890)
366.	(1856)	539.	(1809, 1821)
380.	(1889)	541.	(1849)
381.	(1842)	543.	(1885?)
383.	(1841)	544.	(1891)
384.	(1839)	547.	(1894?)
385.	(1851)	551.	(1887)
392.	(1846-48)	562.	(1846-48)
393.	(1853?)	565.	(1841)
394.	(1841-48)	569.	(1808-16)
398.	(1848)	570.	(1868)
404.	(1846)	579.	(1830-48)
405.	(1892)	581.	(1874)
406.	(1876)	585.	(1890)
411.	(1873 to Jan. 1874)	586.	(1867)
413.	(1877)	595.	(1836)
414.	(1903)	599.	(1887)
421.	(1846-48)	600.	(1861-62)
423.	(1843-44)	601.	(1886)
427.	(1887)	602.	(1875)
429.	(1892)	606.	(1882-1960)
437.	(1878)	608.	(1847)
439.	(1845)	616.	(late 19th century)
440.	(1844)	617.	(1898)
441.	(1840-50)	618.	(1893)

Number of Books Published in the United States Each Year
in English, Dealing with Latin America, 1840-1900

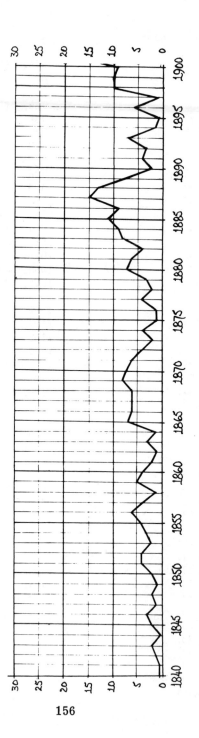

Number of Books Published in the United States
Each Year in English, Dealing with Latin America,
1900-1940

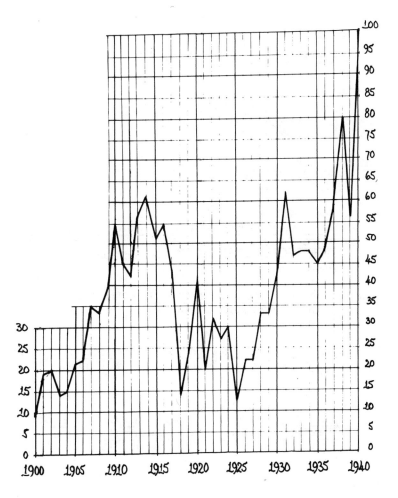

SELECTED LIST OF REFERENCES
Containing Information about
Nineteenth Century Books and Authors

Adams, Oscar Fay (1855-1919)
A Dictionary of American Authors. Boston and
New York: Houghton, Mifflin, 1897. viii, 444p.

Alceda, Antonio de
The Geographical and Historical Dictionary of the
West Indies. London: 1812-15. 5 volumes.
(translated from Spanish.)

The American Catalog of Books [published in the United
States, 1861-1910]. New York: Peter Smith, 1938-
41. 15 volumes.

Ames, John Griffith
Comprehensive Index to the Publications of the United
States Government, 1881-1893. Washington: Govern-
ment Printing Office, 1905. A continuation of B. P.
Poore (below).

Annual American Catalogue, 1886-1910. New York: H. W.
Wilson, 1887-1911. 25 volumes.

The Bancroft Library of the University of California Catalog
of Printed Books. Boston: G. K. Hall, 1964. 22
volumes.

Bartlett, John Russell (1805-86)
Bibliographical Notices of Rare and Curious Books
Relating to America in the Library of the Late John
Brown. Providence: The Library, 1875-82. 2
volumes.

Bauer, Andrew
The Hawthorn Dictionary of Pseudonyms. New York:
Hawthorn Books, 1971. viii, 312p.

References   159

Bayitch, S. A.
    Latin America and the Caribbean. A Bibliographical
    Guide to Works in English. Coral Gables: University
    of Miami Press, 1967. xxviii, 942p.

Bibliographie Hispanique, 1905-1915. New York: Hispanic
    Society of America, 1909-15. 11 volumes.

Bibliotheca Americana. London: Maggs Brothers, 1922-
    30. 9 parts.

Bibliotheca Americana. Catalogue of the John Carter
    Brown Library in Brown University. New York:
    Kraus Reprints, 1961. 3 volumes.

Blake, Wilson Wilberforce (1850-1918)
    Ninth Catalogue of the Second Hand Books ... Relat-
    ing Chiefly to Spanish America. Mexico, 1910.

Borba de Moraes, Rubens (b. 1899)
    Bibliographica Braziliana [1504-1900]. Amsterdam:
    Colibris, 1958. 2 volumes.

British Books in Print [published 1874-1961]. London: J.
    Whitaker and Son, 1966. 2 volumes.

Brown, J. H. (editor)
    Lamb's Biographical Dictionary of the United States.
    Boston: Federal Book Co., 1900-1903. 2 volumes.

Buck, Solon Justice (1884-1962)
    Travel and Description 1765-1865. Springfield:
    Illinois State History Library, 1914. xi, 514p.

Burke, William Jeremiah and William D. Howe
    American Authors and Books [1640-1940]. New York:
    Gramercy Publishing Co., 1943. ix, 858p.; revised
    edition, New York: Crown, 1962.

Butterworth, Hezekiah (1839-1905)
    Traveller Tales of the Pan American Countries.
    Boston: D. Estes and Co., 1902. 289p.; reprinted,
    New York: A. M. S. Press, 1971.

Canning House Library. The Hispanic Council [author and
    subject catalog]. Boston: G. K. Hall, 1967. 4
    volumes.

A Catalog of Books Represented by the Library of Congress
      Printed Cards Issued to July 31, 1942.   Ann Arbor:
      Edwards Brothers, 1942-72.   167 volumes; several
      supplements printed.

Catalog of the Latin American Collection of the University
      of Texas, Austin. Boston: G. K. Hall, 1969.   31
      volumes; supplement, 1971, 5 volumes.

Catalog of the Oliveira Lima Library of the Catholic Uni-
      versity of America, Washington, D. C.   Boston:
      G. K. Hall, 1970.   2 volumes.

Catalog of the Public Documents of Congress and all
      Departments of the United States Government for the
      Period March 4, 1893 to December 31, 1940.
      Washington: Government Printing Office, 1896-
      1945.   25 volumes.   This continues J. G. Ames.

A Catalogue of Geography, Voyages, Travels, Americana.
      London: Bernard Quaritch, 1895.   200p.

Catalogue of Parliamentary Papers, 1801-1920.   London:
      King, 1904-22.   3 volumes.

The Century Dictionary and Cyclopedia... [volume XI is
      Cyclopedia of names].   New York: Century Co.,
      1911; revised 1913.

Chalmers, Alexander (editor)
      General Biographical Dictionary.   London: Whitaker,
      1812-17.   32 volumes.

Checklist of United States Public Documents 1789-1909.
      Washington: Government Printing Office, 1911.
      1707p.   (3rd revised edition)

Church, Elihu Dwight (1835-1908)
      A Catalogue of Books Relating to the Discovery and
      Early History of North and South America [volume
      V covers period 1753-1884].   New York: Dodd,
      Mead, 1907.   5 volumes.   (Reprinted: New York,
      Peter Smith, 1951.)

Clements, William L. (1861-1934)
      The William L. Clements Library of Americana at

the University of Michigan.   Ann Arbor: The University, 1923.   xii, 228p.

Condon, Josiah (1789-1855) (editor)
The Modern Traveler [travel accounts in various countries of world].   London, 1824-30.   30 volumes.

Cook, Dorothy E. and Estelle A. Fidell
Fiction Catalog; A Subject, Author and Title List of 3400 Works of Fiction in the English Language.   New York: H. W. Wilson, 1951.   561p.

Cooper, Gayle (compiler)
A Checklist of American Imprints [for 1830].   Metuchen: Scarecrow Press, 1972.   493p.

Cooper, M. Frances (compiler)
A Checklist of American Imprints.   Title Index 1820-29.   Metuchen: Scarecrow Press, 1972.   562p.

Coulter, Edith and Melanie Gerstenfeld
Historical Bibliographies.   A Systematic and Annotated Guide.   Berkeley: University of California, 1935.   xii, 206p.

Courtney, William Prideaux (1845-1913)
The Secrets of our National Literature; Chapters on the History of the Anonymous and Pseudonymous Writings of our Countrymen.   London: A. Constable, 1908.   vii, 255p.

Cowan, Robert Ernest
Bibliography of the History of California, 1510-1930. San Francisco: Nash, 1933.   3 volumes.

Cox, Edward Godfrey
A Reference Guide to the Literature of Travel... [volume II, the New World].   Seattle: University of Washington, 1935-49.   3 volumes.

Crone, Gerald Roe (editor)
The Explorers.   Great Adventurers Tell their own Stories of Discoveries.   New York: Crowell, 1963. xxii, 361p.

Crowley, Ellen and Robert C. Thomas (editors)
Reverse Acronyms and Initialisms Dictionary.   Detroit: Gale Research, 1972.   xv, 484p.

Cumulative Book Index. World List of Books in English
[continues Books in Print]. New York: R. R. Bowker,
1928ff. Includes reprints.

Cundall, Frank (1858-1937)
Bibliographica Jamaicaensis [references in the Institute of Jamaica]. Kingston: Institute of Jamaica,
1902. v, 83p. (Reprinted: New York, Burt Franklin, 1971.)

Cundall, Frank
Bibliography of the West Indies [except Jamaica].
Kingston: Institute of Jamaica, 1909. vi, 179.
(Reprinted: New York, Johnson Reprint Corp.,
1971.)

Cushing, Helen Grant and Adah V. Morris (editors)
Nineteenth Century Readers' Guide to Periodical
Literature [1890-99]. New York: H. W. Wilson,
1944. 2 volumes.

Cushing, William (1811-95)
Anonyms; a Dictionary of Revealed Authorship.
Cambridge: W. Cushing, 1889. 829p. (Reprinted:
Waltham, Mark Press, 1963.)

Cushing, William
Initials and pseudonyms. A Dictionary of Literary
Disguises. New York: Crowell, 1885-88. 2
volumes. (Reprinted: Waltham, Mark Press, 1963.)

Cutright, Paul Russell (b. 1897)
The Great Naturalists Explore South America. New
York: Macmillan, 1940. xii, 340p. (Reprinted:
Freeport, Books for Libraries, 1968.)

Danforth, G. F. and M. E. Potter (editors)
United States Catalog; Books in Print, 1899. Min-
neapolis: H. W. Wilson, 1900. 2 volumes.

Decoud, John M.
A List of Books, Magazine Articles and Maps Relating to Paraguay [1638-1903]. Washington: Government Printing Office, 1904. 53p.

Delaney, John J. and James Edward Tobin
Dictionary of Catholic Biography. Garden City:
Doubleday, 1961. xi, 1245p.

Deuel, Leo
Conquistadores without Swords. Archaeologists in
the Americas. New York: St. Martin's Press,
1967. xxii, 647p.

Diccionario Encyclopedio Hispano-Americana. Barcelona:
1887-1900. 28 volumes.

A Dictionary Catalog of American Book Printing from the
Seventeenth through the Nineteenth Centuries. Westport: Greenwood, 1971; reprint.

Dictionary Catalog of the Edward E. Ayer Collection of
Americana and American Indians in the Newberry
Library. Boston: G. K. Hall, 1961. 15 volumes.

Dobell, Bertram
Catalogue of Books Printed for Private Circulation....
London: Dobell, 1906. 238p.

Duyckinck, Everet Augustus (1816-78)
Cyclopedia of American Literature [to 1875]. Philadelphia: T. E. Zell, 1875. 2 volumes.

Economic Literature of Latin America. Cambridge: Har-
vard University, 1935-6. 2 volumes.

English Catalogue of Books Published 1801-1930. London:
S. Low, 1864-1931. 13 volumes.

Felid Cruz, Guillermo
Notas para una bibliografía sobre viajeros relativos
a Chile [includes 154 English and American travelers
in Part 3]. Santiago: Editorial Universitaria, 1965.

Foley, P. K.
American Authors, 1795-1895. A Bibliography of
First and Notable Editions. New York: Milford
House, 1969, first edition 1897.

Freyre, Gilberto (b. 1900)
    "Social life in Brazil in the middle of the nineteenth
    century, " [references in several languages, p. 629-
    30]. Hispanic American Historical Review, Novem-
    ber 1922. 597-630p.

Gardiner, Clinton Harvey
    "Foreign traveler's accounts of Mexico, 1810-1910"
    [394 items]. Americas, January 1952. 321-51p.

Geigel y Zenón, José and Abelardo Morales Ferrer
    Bibliográfica puertorriqueña, escrita en 1492-1894.
    Barcelona, 1934.

General Alphabetical Index to the Bills, Reports, Estimates,
    Accounts, Printed by Order of the House of Com-
    mons and the Papers Presented by Command, 1801-
    1929. London: Stationery Office, 1853-1931. 7
    volumes.

A General Catalogue of Books offered ... for sale by
    Bernard Quaritch. London: G. Norman, 1868.
    viii, 1130p. Supplements: 1874, 2 vols., x, 1889p.;
    1875, 2 vols., iv, 1672p.; 1880, 3 vols., x, 2395p.;
    1880-92, 16 vols.

General Catalogue of Printed Books [in British Museum 1455-
    1955]. New York: Readex Microprint, 1967. 27
    volumes.

General Index to Sessional Papers Printed by Order of the
    House of Lords or Presented by Special Command
    [1801-85]. London: Eyre, 1860-86. 3 volumes.

Gillett, Theresa and Helen McIntyre
    Catalog of Luso-Brazilian Material in the University
    of New Mexico Libraries. Metuchen: Scarecrow
    Press, 1970. 961p.

Goldsmith, Peter Hair (1866-1926)
    A Brief Bibliography of Books in English, Spanish
    and Portuguese Relating to the Republics Commonly
    Called Latin America. New York: Macmillan, 1915.
    xix, 107p.

Goveia, Elsa V.
      A Study on the Historiography of the British West
      Indies.   Mexico, 1956.

Gregg, H. C.
      "Early Victorian Travellers, " Blackwood's Magazine,
      August 1897.   181-93p.

Griffin, Charles C. (editor)
      Latin America. A Guide to the Historical Literature.
      Austin: University of Texas Press, 1971.   xxx,
      700p.

Gropp, Arthur E.
      A Bibliography of Latin American Bibliographies.
      Metuchen: Scarecrow Press, 1968.   528p.   Sup-
      plement, 1971, 277p.

Haferkorn, Henry E.
      The War with Mexico, 1846-48.   A Select Bibli-
      ography with Description and Critical Annotations.
      Washington: U. S. Engineering Bureau, 1914.
      xxviii, 93p.   (Reprinted: New York, Argonaut,
      1965.)

Halkett, Samuel (1814-71) and John Laing (1809-80) (editors)
      Dictionary of Anonymous and Pseudonymous English
      Literature.   Boston: Lockwood, Brooks and Co. ,
      1882-88.   4 volumes.   (Reprinted: New York,
      Haskell House, 1971, with additions.   7 volumes.)

Hamilton, Charles Granville
      "English speaking travelers in Brazil, 1851-81, "
      Hispanic American Historical Review, November
      1960.   533-47p.

Hasse, Adelaide Rosalie (b. 1868)
      Reports of Explorations Printed in the Documents
      of the United States Government.   Washington:
      Government Printing Office, 1899.   90p.

Havlice, Patricia Pate
      Index to American Author Bibliographies.   Me-
      tuchen: Scarecrow Press, 1971.   204p.

Haynes, John Edward
    Pseudonyms of Authors, including Anonyms and
    Initialisms. Detroit: Gale Research, 1969.   112p.
    (first edition 1882)

Hirshberg, Herbert Simon and Carl Herman Melinat (editors)
    Subject Guide to United States Government Publica-
    tions.   Chicago: American Library Association,
    1947.   228p.

History of the Americas Collection [Dictionary Catalog of
    the New York Public Library].   Boston: G. K. Hall,
    1961.   28 volumes.

Humphreys, R. A.
    Latin American History.   A Guide to the Literature
    in English.   London: Oxford University Press, 1958.
    xiv, 197p.

Hunt, William
    "Travelers and travel literature of the nineteenth
    century, " Explorers Journal, September 1968.
    197-206p.

Hyamson, Albert Montefiore (b. 1875)
    A Dictionary of Universal Biography of all Ages and
    of all Peoples.   New York: E. P. Dutton, 1951.
    xii, 679p.

Index Translationum [International bibliography of transla-
    tions].   Paris: International Institute of Intellectual
    Cooperation, 1932-34.   10 parts.

Johnson, Allen and Dumas Malone (editors)
    Dictionary of American Biography.   New York:
    Scribner's, 1928-37.   20 volumes.

Jones, Cecil Knight (b. 1872)
    A Bibliography of Latin American Bibliographies.
    Washington: Government Printing Office, 1942.
    307p.   (Reprinted: New York, Greenwood, 1969.)

Jones, Cecil Knight
    Hispanic American Bibliographies.   Baltimore: His-
    panic American Historical Review, 1922.   Supple-
    ments, 1926ff.

References   167

Jones, L. E. (compiler)
     The American Catalogue [authors and titles 1876-
     1900]. New York: Peter Smith, 1941. 10 volumes.

Jones, Tom B.
     South America Rediscovered [travelers 1810-70].
     Minneapolis: University of Minnesota, 1949. ix,
     285p.

Jones, Willis Knapp
     Latin American Writers in English Translation. A
     Classified Bibliography. Washington: Pan American
     Union, 1944. (Reprinted: Detroit, Blaine Ethridge,
     1972.)

Kaiser, John Boynton
     The National Bibliographies of the South American
     Republics. Boston: Boston Book Co., 1913. 20p.

Kelly, James (compiler)
     The American Catalogue of Books [published in the
     United States, January 1861 to January 1871]. New
     York: Peter Smith, 1938. 2 volumes.

Keniston, Hayward (b. 1883)
     List of Works for the Study of Hispanic American
     History. New York: Hispanic Society of America,
     1920. xviii, 451p.

Kennedy, James, W. A. Smith and A. F. Johnson (editors)
     Dictionary of Anonymous and Pseudonymous English
     Literature. Edinburgh: Oliver and Boyd, 1926-34.
     7 volumes; with supplements, 1956, 1962.

Kunitz, Stanley Jasspon (b. 1905) (editor)
     British Authors of the Nineteenth Century. New
     York: H. W. Wilson, 1936. 677p.

Lawson, William Thornton
     Essay on the Literature of the Mexican War. New
     York: Columbia College, 1882. 21p.

Leclerc, Charles (1843-89)
     Bibliotheca Americana. Paris: Maisonneuve et Cie.,
     1867. vii, 467p. Supplements: 1878, 1881, 1887.

168   References

List of Printed Books in the Library of the Hispanic Society
     of America.   New York: Hispanic Society of America,
     1910.   20 volumes.

List of Works ... Relating to Mexico.   New York: New
     York Public Library, 1919.   x, 186p.

List of Works Relating to the West Indies.   New York:
     New York Public Library, 1912.   392p.

MacShane, Frank (editor)
     Impressions of Latin America.   Five Centuries of
     Travel.   New York: Morrow, 1963.   332p.

Martin, John
     Bibliographical Catalogue of Privately Printed Books.
     London: J. Van Voorst, 1854.   593p.   (second
     edition)

Medina, José Toribio (1852-1930)
     Biblioteca Hispano-Americana [1493-1810].   Santiago:
     The Author, 1898-1907.   7 volumes.

Mellet, Julián
     Viajes por el interior de la América Meridional
     [1808-20].   Santiago: Cámara Latinoamericana del
     Libro, 1921?   289p.

Mill, Hugh Robert
     Catalogue of the Library of the Royal Geographical
     Society.   London: John Murray, 1895.

National Cyclopedia of American Biography.   New York:
     White, 1892-1933.   23 volumes.   Supplement, 4
     volumes, 1935; 49 volumes edition, 1921-66.

Naylor, Bernard
     Accounts of Nineteenth Century South America.   An
     Annotated Check List of Works by British and United
     States Observers.   London: Oxford University
     Press, 1969.   iv, 80p.

Nilon, Charles H.
     Bibliography of Bibliographies in American Literature.
     New York: R. R. Bowker, 1970.   483p.

O'Neill, Edward Hayes
Biography by Americans, 1658-1936. Philadelphia:
University of Pennsylvania Press, 1939. 465p.

Parker, Franklin D.
"Nineteenth century travel impressions; the United
States and Guatemala, " Inter-American Review of
Bibliography, October-December 1968. 400-14p.

Peddie, Robert Alexander
Subject Index of Books Published up to and Including
1880. London: Grafton, 1933. 745p.

Pedreira, Antonio S.
Bibliografía puertoriquena [1493-1930]. Madrid,
1932. xxxii, 707p.

Phillips, Lawrence Barnett
Dictionary of Biographical References. London:
S. Low, 1899 and Philadelphia: Gebbie, 1889.
1038p.

Phillips, Philip Leo (1857-1924)
A List of Books, Magazine Articles and Maps Relating to Brazil 1800-1900. Washington: Government Printing Office, 1901. 145p.

Phillips, Philip Lee
A List of Books, Magazine Articles and Maps Re-
lating to Central America 1800-1900. Washington:
Government Printing Office, 1902. 109p.

Phillips, Philip Lee
A List of Books, Magazine Articles and Maps Re-
lating to Chile. Washington: Government Printing
Office, 1903. 110p.

Pinkerton, John (1857-1826)
Catalogue of Books of Voyages and Travels [volume
17 covers early nineteenth century]. London,
1808-14. 17 volumes.

Poole, William Frederick and William J. Fletcher (editors)
Poole's Index to Periodical Literature [1802-1906].
Gloucester: Peter Smith, 1963. 6 volumes. (first
edition, 1882-1908.)

Poore, Benjamin Perley
    A Descriptive Catalogue of the Government Publica-
    tions of the United States, September 5, 1774 to
    March 4, 1881. Washington: Government Printing
    Office, 1885. 1392p.

Poppino, R. E.
    Brazil, Land and People [bibliography p. 330-37].
    London: Oxford University Press, 1968. viii, 370p.

Potter, Marion (editor)
    United States Catalog. Books in Print, 1902. Min-
    neapolis: H. W. Wilson, 1903. 2150p.

The Publishers' Trade List Annual, 1972 [for reprints of
    nineteenth century books]. New York: R. R. Bowker,
    1972 and previous years.

Ragatz, Lowell J.
    A Guide for the Study of British Caribbean History,
    1763-1834.... Washington: Government Printing
    Office, 1932. (Reprinted: New York, Da Capo Press,
    1970. viii, 725p.)

Reading List on Cuba and the Present War with Spain [books
    and periodical articles]. Buffalo: The Library, 1898.
    16p.

"Recent books in English on description and travel in Latin
    America." Washington: Pan American Union, 1929.
    14p. mimeographed.

Reeder, Russell P.
    The Story of the Mexican War [with bibliography].
    New York: Meredith Press, 1967. vii, 184p.

Rhoades, Elizabeth R.
    Foreigners in Southern California during the Mexican
    Period. San Francisco: R. and R. Research Asso-
    ciates, 1971. (first edition 1924)

Rich, Obadiah (1777-1850)
    Bibliotheca Americana Nova [volume 2 covers years
    1801-44]. London, 1835-46. 2 volumes. (Reprinted:
    New York, Burt Franklin, 1963.)

Riches, Phyllis M.
Analytical Bibliography of Universal Collected Biography, Comprising Books Published in the English
Tongue in Great Britain and Ireland, America and
the British Dominions. London: Library Association,
1934. 709p.

Roorbach, Orville Augustus (1803-61)
Bibliotheca Americana. Catalogue of American Publications 1820-61. New York: Roorbach, 1852-61.
4 volumes.

Sabin, Joseph (1821-82)
Bibliotheca Americana. A Dictionary of Books Relating to America. New York: J. Sabin and Son,
1868-1936. 29 volumes. (Reprinted: Metuchen,
Scarecrow Press, 1966.)

Shand, Alexander Innes
"Travelling naturalists in the New World," Bibliographical Quarterly, October 1892. 445-75p.

Sharp, Harold S. (editor)
Handbook of Pseudonyms and Personal Nicknames.
Metuchen: Scarecrow Press, 1972. 2 volumes.

Shaw, Ralph R. and Richard H. Shoemaker
American Bibliography 1801-19. Metuchen: Scarecrow Press, 1958. 22 volumes.

Sibley, Marilyn McAdams
Travelers in Texas 1761-1860. Austin: University
of Texas Press, 1966. viii, 236p.

Smith, Alfred Russell
Bibliotheca America. Catalogue of a Valuable Collection of Books and Pamphlets Illustrating the History and Geography of North and South America and
the West Indies. London: A. R. Smith, 1871. vii,
234p.

Smith, H. F.
"A bibliography of American traveller's books about
Cuba published before 1900," Americas, April 1966.
404-12p.

Smith, Justin Harvey
    The War with Mexico [extensive bibliography in
    volume 2]. New York: Macmillan, 1919. 2
    volumes. (Reprinted: Gloucester, Peter Smith,
    1963.)

Spain and Spanish America in the Libraries of the Univer-
    sity of California. A Catalog of Books. Berkeley:
    University of California, 1928-30. 2 volumes.

Stephen, Leslie and Sidney Lee (editors)
    Dictionary of National Biography. London: Smith,
    Elder, 1885-1900. 63 volumes. Supplements, 1901,
    1912, etc.

Stevens, Henry (1819-86)
    Bibliotheca Historica. Boston: Houghton, 1870.
    xiv, 234p.

Stevens, Henry
    Catalogue of the American Books in the Library of
    the British Museum [as of December 1856]. London:
    H. Stevens, 1866. 4 parts.

Stevens, Henry
    Historical Nuggets. Bibliotheca Americana. London:
    Whittingham and Wilkins, 1857-85. 3 volumes.

Still, Bayrd
    The West. Contemporary Records of American Ex-
    pansion Across the Continent, 1607-1890. Magnolia,
    Mass.: Peter Smith, 1961. 279p.

Stonehill, Charles Archibald (b. 1900), Andrew Block,
    and H. W. Stonehill
    Anonyms and Pseudonyms. London: The Author,
    1926-7. 4 volumes. (Reprinted: New York, Mil-
    ford House, 1969.)

Subject Guide to Books in Print, 1972. New York: R. R.
    Bowker, 1972. 2 volumes and earlier editions.

Thwaites, Ruben Gold (editor)
    Early Western Travels, 1748-1846.... Cleveland:
    A. H. Clark, 1904-7. 32 volumes. (Reprinted:
    New York, 1965.)

Toro, Josefina del
    A Bibliography of the Collective Biography of
    Spanish America. Río Piedras: University of
    Puerto Rico, 1938. vi, 140p.

Trask, David F., Michael C. Meyer, and Rober R. Trask
    A Bibliography of United States--Latin American Re-
    lations since 1810. Lincoln: University of Nebraska
    Press, 1968. xxxii, 441p.

Trifilo, Samuel
    "A Bibliography of British travel books on Argentina,
    1810-60," Americas, October, 1959. 133-43p.

Trifilo, Samuel
    "British accounts on Argentina before 1810," Journal
    of Inter-American Studies, July, 1960. 239-56p.

Trifilo, Samuel
    "Early nineteenth century British travelers in Chile.
    Impressions of Santiago and Valparaiso," Journal
    of Inter-American Studies, July, 1969. 391-424p.

Trübner, Nikalaus
    Trübner's Bibliographical Guide to American Litera-
    ture. A Classed List of Books [published in the
    United States for "last 40 years"]. London: Trübner,
    1859. 554p.

Union Catalog of the Library of Congress [to Hannemann].
    London: Marsell, 1968-72. 229 volumes.

Viajeros en Chile, 1817-47. Santiago: Cámara Latinoameri-
    cana del Libre, 1948? 254p.

Voyages and Travels in all Parts of the World [catalog].
    London: Maggs Brothers, 1942-52. 3 volumes.

Wallace, William Stewart (b. 1884) (compiler)
    A Dictionary of North American Authors Deceased
    before 1950. Toronto: Ryerson Press, 1951.
    (Reprinted: Detroit, Gale, 1968. viii, 525p.)

Watson, Gayle Hudgens
  Colombia, Ecuador and Venezuela. Annotated Guide
  to Reference Materials in the Humanities and Social
  Sciences. Metuchen: Scarecrow Press, 1971.
  279p.

Watson, George
  The New Cambridge Bibliography of English Litera-
  ture [volume 3 covers 1800 to 1900]. Cambridge:
  At the University Press, 1969. 3 volumes.

Wauchope, Robert
  They Found the Buried Cities. Exploration and Ex-
  cavation in the American Tropics. Chicago: University of Chicago Press, 1965. viii, 382p.

Webster's Biographical Dictionary. A Dictionary of Names
  of Noteworthy Persons. Springfield: G. and C.
  Merriman, 1967. xxxvi, 1697p.

White's Conspectus of American Biography. New York:
  J. T. White Co., 1937. vii, 455p. (second edition)

Whitney, James Lyman (1835-1910)
  Catalogue of the Spanish Library and of the Portu-
  guese Books Bequeathed by George Ticknor to the
  Boston Public Library. Boston: Rockwell and
  Churchill, 1890. 71p.

Wilgus, A. Curtis
  Histories and Historians of Hispanic America. New
  York: Cooper Square Publishers, 1965. xii, 144p.;
  first edition, 1942.

Willard, Frances Elizabeth (1839-98) and Mary A. Livermore
  A Woman of the Century [1470 biographical sketches
  of United States women]. Buffalo: Charles Wells
  Moulton, 1893. 812p.

Wilson, J. G. and John Fiske
  Appleton Cyclopedia of American Biography. New
  York: Appleton, 1887-1900. 7 volumes.